# Origins of
# American
# Marxism

# the Origins of American Marxism

From the Transcendentalists to De Leon

David Herreshoff

original hardback title: American Disciples of Marx

A MONAD PRESS BOOK distributed by:
PATHFINDER PRESS, NEW YORK

Copyright © 1967 by Wayne State University Press
Detroit, Michigan 48202.
All rights reserved

No part of this book may be reproduced without formal
permission

First Edition, 1967
First Monad Paperback Edition, 1973

Published by Monad Press
for the Anchor Foundation, Inc.

Distributed by
Pathfinder Press, Inc.
410 West Street
New York, N.Y. 10014

Library of Congress Catalog Card Number 73-81701
Manufactured in the United States of America

In memory of Professor Leo Stoller. We had planned to collaborate on further studies of early labor radicalism in America.

# contents

# illustrations

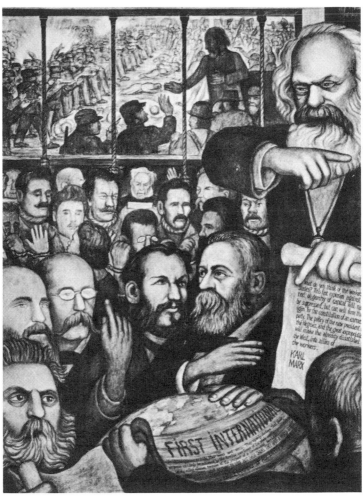

Panel from Diego Rivera mural showing Karl Marx addressing
American radicals while the banner of the First International
is unfurled around the globe. Johann Most occupies lower
left-hand corner; above, from left to right: Terence V. Powderly,
William Sylvis, Friedrich Engels. In the background, police
fire on workers in Chicago's Haymarket.

# Chapter 1

# Marx and the Transcendentalists

The history of the United States was not worth much study, thought G. W. F. Hegel. "America," he said, "has shown, and continues to show itself to be physically and spiritually feeble," a place "removed from the territories in which world history has occurred," and "a land of the future." Nothing important was going on in America and nothing important was going to happen there for a long time. Events which could make for significant changes in the human condition there, he suggested, were ruled out by the frontier.

It was the lack of a frontier, in the American sense of the word, which had made history possible in the old world. What would have happened in France, Hegel wondered, if France during his lifetime had possessed a frontier, if Germany had still been the forest wilderness it had been in Roman times? He supposed that "the French Revolution would probably not have taken place." The plebeians of Paris would probably have crossed the Rhine to clear ground and raise log cabins in Hegel's hypothetical German wilderness, instead of staying in Paris to pull down the Bastille and set up the guillotine. As long as an "untamed wilderness rules all imaginations" in the United States, meaningful politics would remain an old world monopoly. As long as the American mind was filled with the west, "what now passes for politics in America" would be "only a kind of festival engaged in for the fun of it." The American celebrants of the joyous, irrational, impotent rituals of American politics would continue to posture in a void until "social differentiation has occurred—when wealth and poverty loom large and a great multitude can no longer satisfy their needs in their accustomed manner." The United States, Hegel predicted, could expect to be spared such a social crisis for a very long time because "in the settling of new land it has a virtually permanent way of avoiding it. The constant flow of people to the plains of the Mississippi overcomes unrest at its principal sources and stabilizes existing conditions." Finally, however, the wide-open spaces would be gone, the farming population would cease to grow, Americans would "turn from agriculture to urban livelihoods, establish a compact society, and arrive at the necessity for an organized state."[1] But Hegel believed he would not live to see an American society and state in which politics would be rational rather than ritualistic, in which the wills of men and the platforms of parties would count for something. That is why he concluded that he could afford to pay very little attention to America.

Among Hegel's disciples one at least accepted the master's view of America as "stateless" and historically insignificant. For Ferdinand Lassalle it was scarcely possible to speak of an American state, since in the United States "only individual freedom and the limited interests of bourgeois society are taken care of, and the Americans lack art and science, as their political life lacks every higher objective interest." But for Karl Marx, a rebellious Hegelian, such disdainful talk about America was simply "decayed rubbish."[2]

Marx's own early observations about the United States, however, show that he was not completely opposed to the Hegelian outlook on the new world. He saw the same lack of a significant political consciousness in America that the Hegelians saw. For

12

him, the political institutions of the American republic in 1852 typified the "conservative form of life" of bourgeois society. But American conservatism was only one pole in the dialectic of American history; the other pole was the country's economic dynamism. In the United States, as it appeared to Marx in 1852, social classes were "in a constant state of flux"; a shortage of workers was making for greater productivity and, as a result, "the feverishly youthful movement of material production, that has a new world to make its own, has left neither time nor opportunity for abolishing the old spirit world."[3]

The opportunity for abolishing the old spirit world of false consciousness would not confront Americans as long as the frontier and the wilderness fed the American imagination. Until the inevitable disappearance of the frontier, the expansive boldness of America's economy would be accompanied by a conservative timidity of America's mind. This image of America, which Marx derived from Hegel, was the opposite of Frederick Jackson Turner's. Where Turner saw the frontier as the solvent of crusty European ideas and institutions, Marx saw it as their conserver. Consequently, Marx waited eagerly for the end of the frontier while Turner recorded its passing with regret. The end of the frontier for Marx and Turner, as for Hegel before them, spelled the end of America's uniqueness, the beginning of its Europeanization.[4]

If Marx took from Hegel the view that Americans were too busy to think radically and that their preoccupation with personal economic interests would continue while American capitalism still had "a new world to make its own," in what way did he reject Hegel's view? The answer is that Marx could not accept Hegel's dismissal of America as a country where nothing was happening, a country outside history. Marx, the historical materialist, believed that the "feverishly youthful movement of material production" in the United States meant that the country was already acting within history in the middle of the nineteenth century. The first American Marxists were disposed, by Marx's dissent from Hegel, to find American affairs interesting. It was easier for them to avert their gaze from Germany and to focus it on the United States than

13

for those German radicals who, after finding refuge here, continued to view the country through Hegel's spectacles. The Marxists were ready to see more in American politics than the survival of prehistoric ritual.

There is a strong and broad American radical tradition older than Marxism; subjugated men and women have often raised the cry for justice in the United States. Wishing to break the yoke of a ruling class, the white race, or the male sex, Americans have joined movements aimed at completing the unfinished business of 1776. "We will take up the ball of the Revolution where our fathers stopped it," said the agrarian radicals of the New York Anti-Rent movement, "and roll it to the final consummation of freedom and independence of the Masses."⁵ The Anti-Renters were farmers chafing under the feudal dues demanded by the Patroons of the Hudson valley. Negroes, women, and workingmen have used similar words in resistance to race, sex, and class tyranny. The idea of completing the revolution is still current in the country; even presidents give voice to it. "The revolution which began in 1776," said President Kennedy during his first weeks in office, "is not yet finished."⁶

It is indeed not finished from the standpoint of the principal egalitarian movements. There have been four of these: the labor movement—made up of unions, cooperatives, and workers' parties —and the farmers', women's, and Negro movements. All four have sought drastic changes in a society which has subordinated men and women who desired independence and dignity. These movements are literally, inescapably, movements of insubordination. Even when subsiding or stagnant they carry a large potential for social change. The persistence of the subordination they protest against keeps them alive. While white supremacy exists, the Negro freedom movement will not die. Feminism and the farmer and labor movements, in one form or another, will rise and fall to rise again while male supremacy, rural poverty, and the alienation of labor continue to outrage their objects.

Egalitarian movements, to their own undoing, tend to be self-centered. Seldom in good rapport with one another, they frequently begrudge one another's right to exist. The labor radical who is anti-Negro, the abolitionist or Negro leader who is pro-capitalist, the feminist who is for the open shop, and the agrarian who is against women's rights are recurring figures in American history. The movements therefore find it difficult to make alliances among themselves, and much of the momentum of social discontent is dissipated by their rivalries. If two or more of them made common cause they would likely be a shaping force in American politics. On a large scale this has never happened; if it did, the United States would no longer be the exceptionally stable, conservative society it continues to be.

A peculiarity sets the labor movement apart from the other egalitarian movements: workers' organizations are largely composed of people who want to escape from the group they find themselves in. They are not celebrators of proletarian culture. If some workers would like to abolish the wage system, others think of rising individually out of the working class; but one way or the other they would rather not be wage workers. Workingclass self-hatred and the rise of the labor movement are responses to the felt loss of dignity in the work process, which is one of the costs of the industrial revolution. Movements of Negroes, women, and farmers, by contrast, are not necessarily composed of men and women who wish to renounce their ethnic, sexual, or class allegiances.

Implicit in the labor movement is the desire to bring working conditions under the control of the workers, and a tendency to be concerned with social and political issues outside the sphere of work. In a radical upsurge, the desire to achieve workers' control of production and the tendency to take up issues which are not peculiarly working class issues become explicit, and the labor movement approaches what Marxists call "class consciousness"; in periods of consolidation or decline it tends to slough off that consciousness until it becomes difficult to pronounce the words "labor movement" without an ironical intonation. In the United States the approaches to class consciousness have not been close. The American labor movement has not consciously struggled for fundamental alteration in the conditions of work and life. It has been, on the whole, no more than a pressure group whose conscious aims have been limited to what might be obtained under the existing social order. Sometimes American labor has been a subordinate member of a political coalition, as in the Jacksonian and New Deal eras and now again under the Johnson administration; at other times it has pursued its limited aims outside political coalitions. Efforts by Marxists and other radicals to transform the labor movement into a conscious, independent, revolutionary force have not availed.

The Marxist failure to radicalize the labor movement by extending its aims used to be regarded as a peculiarly American phenomenon. It seemed obvious sixty years ago that the socialist movement was much more of a reality in Europe than in the United States. Werner Sombart took this contrast for granted and sought an explanation for it in the American standard of living. American socialism had suffered shipwreck, he suggested, on the reefs of roast beef.[7] But ever since European socialism capitulated to European nationalism in 1914, the weakness of the socialist movement in the United States has appeared less and less to be American exceptionalism. American labor radicals who worked to make America's labor movement resemble Europe's, have had their hopes realized, in a most ironic way. The labor movements of Europe and the United States have arrived at a common ideology. It is not a socialist ideology; it is more anti-communist than anti-capitalist. Its goal is the welfare state. The reform of capitalism, the military budget, and the cold war are the articles of its common creed.

American exceptionalism is dated, but there is a related concept—one might call it Western exceptionalism—which illuminates America's relation to the world. The United States and Western Europe, in Gunnar Myrdal's metaphor, are an exceptional cluster of wealthy islands in a swelling ocean of global poverty.[8] World poverty must be abolished, for there are no dykes which can prevent it from ruining the lives of the happy people of plenty. For the people of the West, altruism and self-interest become the same thing in the face of this threat. As yet there has been no decisive awareness of the coincidence of altruism and self-interest. The inevitable tension between poverty and wealth has been heightened as poor nations have tried to overcome the polarity politically, and rich nations have tried to arrest those efforts militarily. Workers in the West have been indifferent, if not hostile, to revolution in underdeveloped countries. If they remain so, it is difficult to see how a humane and rational Western response can be evoked. Such a response would require acceptance in the West of that socialist vision which has always rejected the existence of wealth in the midst of poverty as immoral. Efforts to win acceptance of that vision in Western labor movements are likely to recur, for the egalitarian dream of 1776 is not dead in its homeland or in the West as a whole.

This book is about the earliest attempts to imbue the American labor movement with the socialist vision. It describes the impact America made on the first Marxists who tried and failed to create an American socialist movement. It focuses on their minds as they strove to master American conditions and to reconcile their theory with the facts of American life. The facts they confronted included an indigenous labor radicalism, the configurations of which are typically represented in the thought of Orestes Brownson. When the first Marxists crossed the Atlantic there was set going in the United States a dialectic between Marxist expectations and American thought and experience which resulted, by the time Daniel De Leon and Eugene Debs came into prominence, in an authentic adaptation of Marxism to America.

My account of this development begins with Brownson because he was an American radical of Marx's generation who managed for a time to give allegiance to the individualist values of transcendentalism, while committing himself to class-struggle labor radicalism. Brownson's radicalism expressed the American desire to "sing the simple, separate person" while "uttering the word democratic, the word en masse." The study of Brownson's radicalism calls attention to the kinship of concepts which have become the opposing shibboleths of the cold war; individualism and socialism, free enterprise and collectivism, Emersonianism and Marxism; and it discloses significant features of the intellectual landscape in which the early American Marxists tried to find a place for their ideas.

17

The socialist and individualist movements of the nineteenth century had common intellectual origins and grew with more or less vigor in Europe and America under the pressure of different national environments: a Marx in that century could only have been seminal in Europe and an Emerson in America. The palpable contrast between Marxist socialism and Emersonian individualism, however, conceals the cognate character of the two schools. The writings of Emerson and of other transcendentalists, such as Thoreau and Brownson, are freighted with elements of an American Marxism. Take, for example, Emerson's perception of his times: "Ours is a Revolutionary Age," wrote Emerson in his journal (1839), "when man is coming back to consciousness." In 1845 Marx remarked that man, having become "conscious of his loss [of self], must revolt against this inhumanity."[9] Both men were concerned with the plight of conscious individuals, and both linked revolution and consciousness while protesting against alienation—the estrangement from self and environment which diminishes man into an object dominated and exploited by external forces. Alienated man was vividly pictured in 1837 by Emerson in "The American Scholar." He decried the dwarfing of men through specialization of function into "so many walking monsters —a good finger, a neck, a stomach, an elbow, but never a man."

Man is thus metamorphosed into a thing, into many things. The planter . . . sinks into the farmer, instead of man on the farm. The tradesman . . . is ridden by the routine of his craft and the soul is subject to dollars. The priest becomes a form; the attorney a statute-book; the mechanic a machine; the sailor a rope of the ship.

The proper human response to alienation is revolution, thought Emerson and Marx. America, Emerson felt in 1844, had had "lessons enough in the futility of criticism." Radicals had "thought and written much on labor and reform, and for all they have written, neither the world nor themselves have got on a step."[10] A few months later Marx asserted that "the philosophers have *interpreted* the world in various ways; the point however is to *change* it." Marx was advocating a "revolutionary practice" by means of which conscious, self-changing men would

18

transform their environment and themselves at the same time.[11] Emerson, too, would seem to have had revolutionary practice in mind when he wrote in 1844 of a "conspiracy" between men and "the designs of the Spirit who has led us hither, and is leading us still . . . into a new and more excellent social state than history has recorded."[12] That Emerson's diction is not Marxist only obscures the proximity of his thought to Marx's.

The intellectual distance between Emerson and Marx is shortest in Emerson's "The Young American" (1844) and the *Communist Manifesto* (1847). In both essays history is seen as an interaction between non-human and human forces: the impact of technology and the economic order and the response of human beings to that impact. Both "The Young American" and the *Manifesto* are controlled by the paradox of a technological revolution which is beneficent but which produces a working class sunk in misery. Emerson perceived this paradox in the growth of the railroads. "The land," he prophesied, "will presently be wrapped in a network of iron. The rage for road-building is beneficent for America. . . . The great political promise of the invention is to hold the Union staunch." The beneficence, however, did not extend to the immigrant laborers who were building the railroads:

> Our hospitality to the poor Irishman has not much merit in it. We pay the poor fellow very ill; To work from dark to dark for sixty or even fifty cents a day is but pitiful wages for a married man. It is a pittance when paid in cash, but when, as generally happens, through the extreme want of one party, met by the shrewdness of the other, he draws his pay in clothes and food, and in other articles of necessity, his case is still worse. . . . Besides, the labor done is excessive; and the sight reminds one of negro-driving. Good farmers and sturdy laborers say that they have never seen so much work got out of a man in a day. Poor fellows![13]

Thoreau soon joined Emerson in celebrating the arrival of the railroad while deploring the condition of its workers. In *Walden* he described the railroad as an institution which "regulates a whole country . . . a fate, an *Atropos,* that never turns aside." It would cost men dearly: "Did you ever think what those sleepers are that underlie the railroad? Each one is a man, an Irishman or a Yankee man. The rails are laid on them, and they are covered with sand, and the cars run smoothly over them. They are sound sleepers, I assure. And every few years a new lot is laid down and run over; so that if some have the pleasure of riding on a rail, others have the misfortune to be ridden upon." Thoreau evoked the lack of consciousness which renders men victims instead of masters of technology when he imagined a workingclass remonstrance against his social criticism. " 'What!' exclaim a million Irishmen starting up from all the shanties of the land, 'is not this railroad which we have built a good thing?' Yes, I answer, *comparatively* good, that is, you might have done worse."[14]

In the *Manifesto* Marx linked technology and human misery in much the same way that Emerson had before him. He credited the bourgeoisie with liberating the productive forces. "It has accomplished wonders far surpassing the Egyptian pyramids, Roman aqueducts, and Gothic cathedrals; it has conducted expeditions that put in the shade all former exoduses of nations and crusades." He condemned the paradox whereby the worker, "instead of rising with the progress of industry, sinks deeper and deeper below the conditions of existence of his own class." He went on to predict the development of a permanent army of the unemployed. The capitalist class becomes "incompetent to assure an existence to its slave within his slavery, because it cannot help letting him sink into such a state, that it has to feed him, instead of being fed by him." Brought to consciousness of their condition by technological change, the workers unite. "And that union, to attain which the burghers of the Middle Ages, with their miserable highways, required centuries, the modern proletarians, thanks to railways, achieve in a few years." Emerson had seen national unity, but Marx saw class unity resulting from the railroad. In the impact of the railroad Marx found support for his optimistic belief that "the dissolution of the old ideas keeps even pace with the dissolution of the old conditions of existence."[15] Pithy Emerson expressed the same belief when he said, in "The Young American," "new thoughts, new things."

Emerson drew a scheme of history in that essay which resembles that of the *Manifesto*. Like Marx, Emerson emphasized the revolutionary significance of modern industry and commerce. "The historian," he predicted, "will see that trade was the principle of Liberty; that trade planted America and destroyed Feudalism; that it makes peace and keeps peace, and it will abolish slavery." But trade has not been an unalloyed good, for it puts "every kind of faculty of every individual that can in any manner serve any person, *on sale* . . . not only produce and manufactures, but art, skill, and intellectual and moral values . . . it would put everything into the market; talent, beauty, virtue, and man himself." In the *Manifesto* Marx chimes in with Emerson:

> The bourgeoisie . . . has left no other nexus between man and man than naked self-interest, than callous "cash payment." . . . It has resolved personal worth into exchange value. . . . It has converted the physician, the lawyer, the priest, the poet, the man of science, into its paid wage labourers.[16]

There was an optimism in the social criticism of Emerson and Marx deriving from their shared sense of the transitoriness of the evils they censured. Every social order, explained Emerson in "The Young American," has its season. "Feudalism had been good," he observed, but

> it was time for it to die, and as they say of dying people, all its faults came out. Trade was the strong man that broke it down and raised a new and unknown power in its place. . . . It calls out all force of a certain kind that slumbered in the former dynasties. It is now in the midst of its career.[17]

That career would inevitably conclude. "We complain of the oppression of the poor, and of the building up of a new aristocracy on the ruins of the aristocracy it destroyed. But the aristocracy of trade has no permanence. . . . and must give way to somewhat broader and better, whose signs are already dawning in the sky." It was not in the sky but in the minds of its victims that Marx detected signs of the demise of the bourgeois order and the dawning of a new society:

> The bourgeoisie cannot exist without constantly revolutionising the instruments of production, and with them the whole relations of society. . . . All that is solid melts into air, all that is holy is pro-

21

faned, and man is at last compelled to face with sober senses his real conditions of life and his relations with his kind.[18]

Although Emerson expected capitalism to last longer than Marx did, there was no basic difference between them about what would replace it. Individualist as he was, Emerson announced in "The Young American" that an age of "beneficent socialism" was on the way. Its harbingers included "the new movements of the civilized world, the Communism of France, Germany and Switzerland; the Trade Unions, the English League against the Corn Laws," and the founders of utopian communities in America. The coexistence in Europe and America of socialist idealism and mass poverty gave promise of revolutionary events:

> Here are the Etzlers and mechanical projectors, who, with the Fourierists, undoubtingly affirm that the smallest union would make every man rich; and, on the other side, a multitude of poor men and women seeking work, and who cannot find enough to pay for their board. The science is confident, and surely the poverty is real. If any means could be found to bring these two together!

"To bring these two together"—to make socialist theory serve the needs of the victims of the industrial revolution—was the very goal Marx was devoting himself to.

Both Emerson and Marx had mixed reactions to the attempts of utopian colonists to practice socialism. To Emerson a socialist community was a logical "continuation of the same movement which made the joint-stock company for manufacturers, mining, insurance, banking." He could accept the substitution of collective for individual enterprise; but the communities he knew, such as Brook Farm and Fruitlands, seemed too rigid and formal in their equalitarianism. "The actual differences of men must be acknowledged, and met with love and wisdom." He feared that "paying talent and labor at one rate" was unrealistic, and he doubted the wisdom of attempts to socialize maternal functions in view of the "objection almost universally felt by such women in the Community as were mothers, to an associate life, to a common table, and a common nursery, etc., setting a higher value on the private family, with poverty, than on association with wealth." Whatever their shortcomings, the socialist experiments were valuable, thought Emerson, "not [for] what they have done, but [for] the revolution which they indicate is on the way."[19]

Marx, in the *Manifesto*, regarded the socialist communities as "necessarily doomed to failure," but like Emerson he valued the pioneering of their founders who provided

> the most valuable materials for the enlightenment of the working class. . . . The practical measures proposed in them—such as the abolition of distinction between town and country, of the family, of the carrying on of industries for the account of private individuals, and of the wage system, the proclamation of social harmony, the conversion of the functions of the state into a mere superintendence of production—all these proposals point solely to the disappearance of class antagonisms. . . .[20]

Those traits of individualistic Yankee transcendentalism congenial to Marxism were recessive in Emerson and the ferment of which he was representative. Emerson maintained his faith in individual regeneration, his conviction that self-culture is a precondition of progressive social action. And while Emerson could speak sympathetically for the underdogs of the American class struggle, he could not see the working class as a revolutionary factor in history. In 1841 he noted in his journal that the privileged few think it "intolerable that Broad Street Paddies and bar-room politicians, the sots and loafers and all manner of ragged and unclean and foulmouthed persons without a dollar in their pockets should control the property of the country and make the lawgiver and the law." But what else than resentment, he wondered, ought the selfish property-owners expect from the mass of the poor?

> They are opposed to you: yes but first you are opposed to them: they, to be sure, malevolently, menacingly, with songs and rowdies and mobs; you cunningly, plausibly, and well-bred; you cheat and they strike; you sleep and eat at their expense; they vote and threaten and sometimes throw stones, at yours.

This is the sympathy of an observer who expects little of significance from the class struggle, for the proletariat Emerson saw was not imbued with the consciousness, discipline and self-confidence a

23

revolutionary class needs. And Emerson saw no other organized or organizable group on the American scene fit to make a revolution.

For Emerson the immediate condition of man—that terrible collection of walking monsters he had described in "The American Scholar"—made it likely that any organized effort would go awry. Once organized, men tend to decline from spontaneity into routinism. "Every project in the history of reform, no matter how violent and surprising, is good when it is the dictate of a man's genius and constitution, but very dull and suspicious when adopted from another." The time would come, he acknowledged, when collective action would have good results; it would come after individuals have acquired a high consciousness of their personal powers. "Men will live, communicate, and plough, and reap, and govern, as by added etherial power, when once they are united." But harmonious cooperation would "be reached by the reverse of the methods" of the utopian socialists—it would be reached by the methods of individualist self-culture. "The union is only perfect when all the uniters are isolated."[21] To Emerson's belief that self-culture must precede the socialist reconstruction of society one may counterpose Marx's belief (affirmed in the "Theses on Feuerbach") in "the coincidence of the changing of circumstances and of human activity or self-changing." Refusing to view self-culture and social change as sequential, Marx placed himself in an intermediary position between Emerson and the socialists Emerson criticized. But Marx's goal was individualistic. In the *Manifesto* he envisions a society in which "the free development of each is the condition for the free development of all."[22]

City and country are often connotative, respectively, of association and isolation. If one views city and country through the eyes of Emerson and Marx, the widest divergence between the agrarian individualism of the American and the industrial socialism of the German is disclosed. Emerson's locus of values was in the land and Marx's was in the city. For Emerson "the land is the appointed remedy for whatever is false and fantastic in our culture . . . The land, with its tranquillizing, sanative influences, is to repair the errors of a scholastic and traditional education, and bring us into just relations with men and things." He deplored the power of the city to "drain the country of the best part of its population."[23] Marx, on the other hand, welcomed the growth of the city and saw the land, not the city, as the cause of what was false and fantastic in culture.[24] He saw the city as the rescuer of men from "the idiocy of rural life."[25]

Both Emerson and Marx looked forward to a new harmony between man and nature in which the split between city and country would be overcome. This goal, thought Marx, would be approached through a struggle between the classes produced by the industrial revolution, a struggle which would be fought principally in the cities. But Emerson's way to utopia lay in an immediate exodus from the city and the transformation of the countryside into a garden: He eagerly awaited events which would "disgust men with cities and infuse into them the passion for country life and country pleasures." Then men would pursue "the most poetic of all occupations," landscape gardening. "How much better when the whole land is a garden, and the people have grown up in the bowers of paradise."[26] This garden of Emerson's resembles the humanized nature Marx described in 1844 in his *Economic and Philosophical Manuscripts*, a nature available only to social man as the bond between individual men.[27] Eight years earlier Emerson had celebrated in "Nature" the subjection of the environment to man, the reduction of all things before man's "victorious thought" and the transformation of the world into "a realized will—the double of man."

Emerson was the representative American radical in the decade during which Marx evolved his outlook. Other men in the transcendentalist movement were closer to Marx than Emerson. One of these was Orestes Brownson, a herald of something akin to Marxism at the red end of the spectrum of American politics, a decade and more before German Marxist refugees arrived in the United States. Brownson looked hopefully toward the American workers in the 1820's and 1830's. His career as a radical, symbolic of the failure of enduring movements of labor radicalism, is a challenge to which American Marxism is a response. Another challenge was presented by the ethnic diversity of America's proletariat.

### GERMAN DISCOVERY OF AMERICA

When Joseph Weydemeyer and Friedrich Sorge, the pioneers of American Marxism, landed in the early fifties, the United States was undergoing a profound change in its ethnic make-up which particularly affected the working class. The transformation was noticed in 1851 by Herman Melville, enabling him to find a metaphor for America in a ship with a polyglot crew. "At the present time," Ishmael declares in *Moby Dick,*

> not one in two of the many thousand men before the mast employed in the American whale fishery, are American born, though pretty nearly all the officers are. Herein it is the same with the American whale fishery as with the American army and military and merchant navies, and the engineering forces employed in the construction of the American Canals and Railroads.

In America's new, foreign-born proletariat the Germans were a sizeable element, outnumbered only by the Irish. The relations between Irish and German immigrants gave American labor and socialist movements special problems and characteristics for decades.

Irishmen coming to the new world were typically absorbed into an inchoate and often fiercely rebellious mass of unskilled laborers and menials. Tenant farmers or craftsmen uprooted from the village and transplanted into the milieu of a dynamic capitalist economy, not more than 10 percent of immigrants from Ireland managed to become farmers in America. For the great majority immigration meant becoming wage workers and settling in slums and railroad shanties. These Irishmen escaped from the landlord and crop-failure only to encounter the tenement owner and the uncertainties and humiliations of industrial and domestic employment in a new setting. To Emerson they were a living refutation of his doctrine of self-reliance: "Hear their stories of their exodus from the old country, and their landing in the new, and their fortunes appear as little under their control as the leaves of the forest around them."[28] But if they sprouted, withered, and fell involuntarily, they did not live and die in vegetable passivity. Sometimes, as in the New York draft riots of 1863, they sounded "the atheist roar of riot" and seemed to represent a relapse of humanity "whole aeons back in nature."[29] At other times the newly proletarianized Irish found within themselves the courage to assert their right to human life in strikes against their new masters. Usually, they were beaten and their unions destroyed by employers, or driven underground and transformed into secret societies.[30]

Germans had an easier passage into American society because they brought skills which kept them out of the mines, mills, and railroad gangs which absorbed the Irish. Among the 200,000 Germans who entered the United States each year during the 1850's, were thousands of joiners, bakers, engravers, upholsterers, gilders, book-binders, and piano-makers. When they took up their tools again after immigrating, they dominated their trades.[31] While skilled German immigrants undoubtedly experienced indignities and privations, they escaped the harsh exploitation endured by unskilled Irish railroad workers, and later on in America's industrial history by the East European ex-peasants who manned the steel, auto, and packing plants.

Fortunately for the Germans, their skills got them jobs in light industries whose owners were too feeble politically and economically to keep the open shop. Small employers could not hire private armies on the scale of the Pinkerton force which Carnegie and Frick sent against the steel workers at Homestead, nor could they expect federal and state police action in their behalf of the sort which broke Debs's American Railway Union at Pullman. As a result largely German trades, like brewing and cigar-making, were securely organized in the United States long before the country's basic industries were penetrated by unions which survived. While German and other skilled workers in the second half of the nineteenth century slowly formed stable unions out of which grew the American Federation of Labor, a largely Irish tidal wave of protest would occasionally loom up out of that ocean of misery that was the unskilled labor force. The urge to protest found expression in the terrorism of the Molly Maguires in the Pennsylvania coal fields in the seventies, the desperation of railroad workers in the St. Louis "Commune" of 1877, and the massive struggles of the AFL's rival, the Knights of Labor.[32]

Ethnic diversity among the workers was an obstacle to progress for American labor unions and parties well into the twentieth century, and the more thoughtful socialists early recognized that it would somehow have to be overcome if American workers were ever to play a socialist role. Friedrich Sorge, for instance, thought that the first step toward an effective labor radicalism would have to be a breaching of the wall between German-American Marxists and the politically unsophisticated Irish-American workers. Sorge thought of the Irish as the most important part of the working class, with Germans, Negroes, and Yankees constituting a series of elements of declining importance.[33] Sorge, Weydemeyer, and their cohorts worked in the tangled milieu of the American working class on the assumption that German socialism could become acculturated in the United States by transforming instinctive Irish labor radicalism into a conscious socialism which would also assemble the German, Negro, and Yankee workers under its banner. Beyond the elementary task of achieving class solidarity in a polyglot proletariat, loomed the problem of discovering a sensible relationship between an emerging labor movement and the agrarian and middle-class radicalism which had been traditional in America. Weydemeyer died before becoming completely familiar with these tasks and problems, but Sorge came to know them in all their vexing complexity.

As Germans and forty-eighters, Weydemeyer and Sorge held many traits in common with their refugee compatriots in America as well as a few uniquely Marxist traits. Both kinds of traits conditioned the effectiveness of the earliest Marxist propaganda effort in the United States. Typical German radical immigrants saw themselves as bearers of culture in a benighted land.[34] Lovers of good wine, they abhorred the "cold water fanatics" of temperance; enjoyers of the relaxed continental Sunday, they were revolted by strict Sabbatarians; proud of their national origins, they loathed Know-Nothing nativists; rationalists and atheists, they scorned the religious enthusiasms of mid-century America; unalloyed democrats, they regarded the American presidency as a monarchical anachronism. German radicals (and conservatives as well) followed the Democratic party before the Republican party

28

was formed because they identified the Whigs as an anti-immigrant force in American politics. When Germans began to join the Republicans in the 1850's, they had to suppress their aversion to the many temperance and Know-Nothing politicos who had come into the new party from the old Whiggery. After the Civil War Germans tended to be for "sound money" and against inflationary issues of greenbacks, even when they were sympathetic to agrarian movements. With a few exceptions, spokesmen for the German community opposed woman suffrage; German liberals and radicals believed that giving women the vote would strengthen the clerical power in American life.

Weydemeyer and Sorge were model forty-eighters in America except that they deviated from the norm in three traits. They were, first, less convinced of German superiority than most German radicals in the United States; in this they were like their predecessor Kriege, although they never idolized the American people as Kriege had. Secondly, Weydemeyer and Sorge never joined the Democratic party, although most Germans were Democrats before the Republican party was founded and many of them returned to the Democratic fold after the Civil War. Thirdly, their anticlericalism did not lead them to oppose votes for women. Of these traits, the first is of greatest significance: it is a mark of the separation of Marxism from its German antecedents, in particular a mark of the independence of Marx from Hegel and from Hegel's less original disciples.

Marx was a revolutionary who repeatedly predicted revolutions which never arrived and the triumph of revolutions which suffered defeat. But he also recognized the unexpected and came to terms with defeat, and was the first prominent forty-eighter to understand that the counter-revolution of 1849 was more than a momentary reverse for the German revolution. The onset of a German and European boom in the fifties convinced Marx that no early resumption of the revolution could be expected.[35] His response to the unexpected return of social tranquility in Germany was to disband the Communist League and turn his attention to his scholarly labors. While other German refugees held themselves in instant readiness to return to the scene of action in full battle array, Marx settled himself in the British Museum. Meanwhile, Joseph Weydemeyer was making himself at home in the United States—and, paradoxically, estranging himself from many of his fellow Germans in New York who could not accommodate themselves to the real situation in Germany. Among those Germans was August Willich, former commander of the *Karlsruhe Freikorps;* while Marx read in the British Museum and Weydemeyer did labor journalism in New York, Willich toured in America addressing German banquets on the theme of the coming struggle for power in the Fatherland. When Willich spoke to a banquet of the New York *Arbeiterverein* in 1853, the utopian communist Wilhelm Weitling presented him with an enormous second-hand sword which, however, was never drawn in behalf of German unity and freedom.[86] Yet the ceremonial sword, a symbol of exile optimism, was far more popular among the Germans than the Marxist pen. Because of his interest in American affairs and disenchantment with German prospects, Weydemeyer found himself isolated in the milieu of German Americans. Weydemeyer wanted to become American and to remain radical, while most other forty-eighters wanted to remain the one *or* become the other. He did not want to be radical only about Germany. His was a difficult aim—to accept America while being a radical critic of American life. The pursuit of that aim by Weydemeyer and Sorge, and later by Daniel De Leon, will be analyzed in the context of the indigenous labor radicalism of Brownson and his successors.

# Chapter 2

# The Anti-Abolitionists:
# Brownson and Kriege

### ORESTES BROWNSON

Inspired by the distress of workers under capitalism in the 1820's and 1830's, Orestes Brownson anticipated much in later American leftism, especially since 1917. If human suffering made Brownson radical, a political dilemma vitiated his radicalism. The dilemma arose from the antagonism between the North's system of wage labor and the South's slavery. Brownson, and all radicals of his generation, had to decide whether the wage system was the worse of the two labor systems, whether it was a lesser evil than slavery and therefore a system he could temporarily accept, or whether to avoid the issue by preferring self-cultivation to politics. In the early 1830's Brownson tried self-culture and would have agreed with Thoreau that "it is hard to have a Southern overseer; it is worse to have a Northern one; but worst of all when you are the slave-driver of yourself."[1] But for most of his years as a radical, Brownson was a strong advocate of political action and sought solutions for the problems of his age in the struggles of parties and classes. He increasingly felt that the American situation was forcing him to choose between unappealing alternatives. This feeling induced exhausting tensions which led him to abandon radicalism in the 1840's. Brownson's career as a labor radical, with its abrupt ending, established an American pattern; since Brownson many American labor radicals have been gored by the dilemma of the lesser evil: how to deal with the enemies of their enemies. Perennially, this dilemma has fragmented American radical movements.

For Brownson politics and religion were always inseparable. He came to radicalism from rural Protestant beginnings. Born in 1803 in Stockbridge, Vermont, Brownson, while a farm boy, was largely self-educated. An earnest seeker for the true faith, he joined the Presbyterian Church in 1822, became a Universalist two years later, and was ordained a Universalist minister in 1826. With his turn from Presbyterianism to religious liberalism, Brownson was attracted to the nascent American labor movement and its first experiments with independent labor politics. Workers' organizations federated in several cities in the late 1820's, and the resulting central labor bodies produced workingmen's parties in Pennsylvania, New York, and New England.[2] When the Workingmen's party of New York was formed in 1828, Brownson (then twenty-five years old) joined it and became a supporter of a comparatively moderate faction in the party headed by Robert Dale Owen and Frances Wright. With Owen and Wright, Brownson opposed a more extreme faction in the Workingmen headed by Thomas Skidmore. The Skidmore faction stood for abolition of the right of inheritance as the means of making a permanent social revolution. Owen and his followers, on the other hand, sought to elevate the workers by establishing free compulsory education. They believed that knowledge, rather than property, is power. Brownson thought they shared the belief of "the whole non-Catholic world . . . in the power of education to redeem society."[3] Both factions of the "Workies," as members of the Workingmen's party were called, viewed themselves as representatives of the "producing classes"—a category taking in farmers and self-employed manufacturers, as well as wage workers. They saw a sharp cleavage in society between producers and accumulators of wealth; the latter class consisted mostly, in their scheme, of merchants and bankers. The Workies tried to make American party lines conform to that cleavage.

Brownson's formal membership in the Workingmen's party lapsed when the organization split during its first year leaving New York laborers with a choice among three groups bearing the Workingmen's label.[4] Brownson, in any case, felt ill-suited by temperament to be a party regular. "The truth is," he explained in his autobiography, "I never was and never could be a party man, or work in the traces of a party."[5] He kept in touch with the Workingmen's movements during the years of Jackson's presidency when some Workies, including Brownson's friend Isaac T. Hecker, tried to keep alive the idea of a labor party independent of the Democrats. These men called themselves the "genuine Democracy" to distinguish themselves from the official Democrats. "Tammany Hall undertook to absorb us when we had grown too powerful to be ignored," relates Hecker. "They nominated a legislative ticket made up half of their men and half of ours. This move was to a great extent successful, but many of us who were purists refused to compromise. . . ."[6]

Brownson gave such efforts sympathy without active support. He had lost enthusiasm for independent workingclass parties and had come to the conclusion that independent labor politics in the United States was doomed to fail because the workingmen

> are neither numerous nor strong enough to get or to wield the political power of the State. . . . The movement we commenced could only excite a war of man against money, and all history and all reasoning in the case prove that in such a war money carries it over man. Money commands the supplies, and can hold out longer than they who have nothing but their manhood. It can starve them into submission.

Giving up the project of a distinct class party, Brownson looked about for a way of inducing "all classes to cooperate for the workingmen's cause."[7] He lost interest at this time in the Owenite proposal for compulsory education as the means of workingclass emancipation, and took up Channing's ideas of personal regeneration through individual effort. His friend Hecker testifies that in the middle 1830's Brownson was "the American Proudhon" and that he gave Saint-Simonian lectures to the Workingmen, "the object being the amelioration of the condition of the most numerous classes of society in the speediest manner."[8] But in the years when he was giving such lectures, a Massachusetts leader of the Workingmen chided Brownson for his indifference to political action.[9]

The cause of the workers kept Brownson's sympathies through the 1830's, although he was sometimes disappointed in the meagerness of the workers' demands. The thought of striking for a ten-hour day, for instance, appalled him. "We never supported the ten-hour system," he explained in 1838,

> but if the mechanics had struck for six hours, instead of ten, we would have supported them to the best of our ability. Six hours is enough for any man to labor in one day, enough for his health, and enough, in a state of society at all approaching a just one, for his worldly prosperity. Man has a mind as well as a body, and should have time to think as well as exercise his limbs.[10]

Brownson's strong sense of the injustice of the workers' lot impelled him to try once more to find in political action the path to a better society. This time he came to politics as a transcendentalist, but he came aware of the panic of 1837 and the misery it spelled for workers. The Workingmen's reform through universal education, and the self-improvement doctrine of Channing, now seemed equally to him to be mockeries. Economic reform, he now believed, was the precondition to a meaningful pursuit of the aims of Owen and Channing. "Give your starving boy a breakfast before you send him to school," he demanded, in effect, of the Owenites; and he advised the advocates of self-culture to offer "your beggar a cloak before you attempt his moral and intellectual elevation."[11] The latter suggestion, addressed to the followers of Channing, was to be seconded by Thoreau when he began his pursuit of the higher laws in *Walden* with an analysis of man's need for food, shelter, clothing, and fuel: "not till we have secured these are we prepared to entertain the true problems of life with freedom and a prospect of success."[12]

Brownson's sense of the practical was infused with the transcendental insight that "society is for man, not man for society," but his was no longer the individualist transcendentalism, for he now urged that "the perfection of the social state is the means" to individual perfection.[13] The time had "come for all predominance of class to end; for Man, the People to rule." Only then would the work of the friends of man "cease to be the melioration of society, and become the perfecting of the individuals of each successive generation. . . . This done and the wish of the workingmen is fulfilled; the visions of the prophets are realized."[14] Inherent in his language is the messianic spirit of Brownson's labor radicalism. Side by side with visionary enthusiasm there was in Brownson a willingness to stare dispassionately at American realities.

Even in a depression the condition of the American workers could not be convincingly evoked by allusions to empty bellies and ragged clothing. Brownson therefore acknowledged a "general increase in wealth throughout the civilized world for the last forty or fifty years." Productivity of labor and the production of goods had "so multiplied as to baffle all efforts at calculation." The standard of living of the workers was obviously higher than that of their fathers and grandfathers at the time of the American Revolution. However, the immiseration of the proletariat was real, Brownson thought, and the need for labor radicalism in the United States genuine:

> The laboring classes most certainly account many things necessaries of life now, which they then accounted its luxuries. But they are not now less poor. Poverty and wealth are merely relative terms. The only true method of judging this matter is to ascertain whether the position of the producer, relatively to that of the accumulator, be higher or lower, than it was at the epoch of the Revolution . . . it is altogether more difficult for the common laborer to maintain the same social position now, than it was fifty years ago. The general style of living has more than kept pace with the increase of wealth.

Brownson hoped that American workers would grow increasingly restive even as they received benefits from the growth of the productive forces. He expected labor radicalism to persist because the movement of society toward affluence would not keep pace with the rising expectations of the workers, who would take more and more things as necessities that their parents had as luxuries. In the long run such a class would not be bribed into conservatism; struggling to embrace the ever elusive, dazzling American style of life, the working class would again and again reach beyond the necessities of the moment.[15]

Such was Brownson's defense of the theory of impoverishment of the workers in a land of plenty. It was a more compelling defense than any which would ignore or deny the reality of rising living standards. At this time, the 1830's, Brownson saw the working class as an embodiment of his transcendental faith in man's ability to prevail over his environment. That ability, he believed, was about to be demonstrated in the United States: "This too is the country in which the noble ideas of man and society, which French and German scholars strike out in their speculations, are first to be applied to practice, realized in institutions." It would have to be here rather than in Europe, because there Europeans

have old institutions to combat; old prejudices to overcome; old castles and churches to clear away . . . and armed soldiery are ready to repulse them. But here is a virgin soil, an open field, a new people, full of the future, with an unbounded faith in ideas, and most ample freedom. Here, if anywhere on earth, may the philosopher experiment on human nature, and demonstrate what man has it in him to be when and where he has the freedom to be himself.

The ideas of Kant and Hegel, refined by the French socialists, were now to shape an imminent social revolution in the United States.[16]

What would the revolution accomplish? Brownson did not give details about the structure of the new society. "I have no plan of a world-reform for you to adopt," he wrote in 1840, "for I have not yet found one that I could adopt myself." None of the schemes for utopia, from Plato to Robert Owen and Fourier, seemed to him "of any great value."[17] Like Marx, Brownson was long on analysis of present society and short on description of future society. Yet Brownson, like Marx, had the principles of the new society firmly in mind. It would be a classless society; it would be bountifully productive; it would humanize the work process by overcoming the opposition between work and play and between head and hand labor; it would not seek to return to a pre-industrial economy but would make use of modern technology; it would not rest on common property, but would not regard private property as inviolable; its ideal worker would not be the yeoman toiling in solitude, but the man engaged in collective labor and enjoying the "encouragement of warm-hearted and enlightened companionship"; and it would establish marriage on the mutual love of social equals, not on property and the subordination of women as in the past.[18]

The new society, Brownson reasoned, would come about through the political struggle of social classes. Having discarded the method of self-culture, he proposed to engage in the politics of the day, keeping "ever in view" the revolutionary goal and judging "the wisdom of every political or legislative measure . . . by its tendency to carry us towards it, or to remove us from it."[19] The immediate task, thought Brownson, was to defend the American Union from the businessmen whose conduct during the depression of 1837 was "threatening the very existence of the republic by its general baseness."[20] The way to defend the Union was to attack economic institutions and policies which served mercantile and manufacturing interests to the detriment of agricultural interests. Translated into party terms this meant that the workers should support the Jacksonian Democracy against the Whigs in order to put themselves in a better position to fight for their own aims. As Brownson saw the class alignment of American politics in 1840,

the interests of landed property combined with those of labor are now arrayed against the banks generally; but if they are successful, it will not be because the interests of labor count for anything; but because the farming and planting interests are stronger than the mercantile and manufacturing interests. The proletaries, though voters in this contest, serve merely to swell the forces of one or the other party . . . they will gain, however, if the landed interests triumph. . . .[21]

37

In Brownson's expectation, the bloc of three classes in the Democratic party—the workers, farmers, and planters—would not survive the final triumph of Jacksonianism over the business community. That triumph would prepare the North for a new revolution in which wage workers, small farmers, and self-employed businessmen would be ranged against all employers of labor, whether rural or urban. There would then be "a deeper question at issue than is commonly imagined; a question which is but remotely touched in your controversies about United States Banks and Sub-Treasuries, . . . free trade and corporations." Their opportunity having been made ready for them by the Jacksonians, the workers would in due course overwhelm their adversaries. "In any contest they will be as two to one, because the large class of proprietors who are not employers, but laborers on their own lands or in their own shops will make common cause with them."[22] The capitalists, having been previously curbed—though not destroyed—by the Jacksonians, would go under in the revolution. America was pregnant with a new society, Brownson believed, because of polarization of wealth and poverty. The frontier, he said, was of dwindling value as a safety-valve for the aggrieved poor since unemployed proletarians lacked the means to migrate westward from the eastern cities to set themselves up as farmers. Besides—this he predicted in 1840!—the unsettled lands would all be taken up by 1890. Sanctioned by the gospel of Christ, though opposed by organized religion,[23] the revolution would make America's political democracy more meaningful by realizing social democracy.[24]

A social democracy, in Brownson's conception, would know neither capitalists nor wage workers. Every man would incorporate the functions of both, and America would thus become a nation of individuals who possess themselves, of citizens who exploit no one and are exploited by no one.[25] One great legislative measure would establish social democracy and bar the way to a return to power of a privileged class: the abolition of the inheritance of property.[26] This measure, which Brownson had opposed in 1828 when he was in the Workingmen's party, would assure each generation of Americans an equal start in life. The final sweeping away of inequality and privilege would be accomplished by the Locofocos, the left wing of the Democratic party.[27]

While Brownson was working out his revolutionary program for the left-wing Jacksonians, he began to experience a pull toward moderation, gradualism, acceptance of the status quo which was entirely at odds with that program. The rightward pull was a consequence of his Democratic politics. He had announced his affiliation to the Democratic party in 1839 in an article devoted to "Democracy and Reform," the thesis of which was that the Democrats, as the movement party in America, were destined to emancipate wage laborers, women, and the slaves once they had torn down the system of class privilege and federal power upheld by the Whigs, the stand-pat party in the country.[28] Since the Democratic Party would ultimately serve the interests of all the egalitarian movements, Brownson reasoned, it was only logical that the radical laborites, the feminists, and the abolitionists should immediately support the Democrats against the Whigs. But, however logical, Brownson's tactic was unacceptable to the abolitionists; for them to enter the Jacksonian Party would have required accommodating themselves to slavery, deferring the struggle for abolition. Opposition to antislavery agitation was the unavoidable price paid by northerners for political alliance with the southern planters. Brownson's involvement with the Democrats therefore thrust him painfully but inevitably into choosing between the abolitionists and the planters.

At the height of his radicalism, Brownson recognized the universality of the egalitarian principle. "We can," he acknowledged in 1838, "legitimate our own right to freedom only by arguments which prove also the negro's right to be free."[29] But in the next breath he went on to argue against the abolitionists' efforts to make the Negro free. The abolitionists, he complained, are impractical, out of step with the times; they did not understand what it means to be politic:

> The question for to-day is the currency question,—not the most interesting question in itself surely, nor a question of the first magnitude; but it is first in the order of time. . . . What will be the question for to-morrow we ask not.

To be a consistent Jacksonian Democrat twenty years before the Civil War, Brownson had to maintain that slavery was not a politically relevant issue in the United States. It was the social make-up of the Jacksonian coalition, far more than the urgency of Jacksonian fiscal policy, which made Brownson oppose the abolitionists. In taking his stand Brownson was the prisoner of his allies. Anyone wishing to coexist in a coalition with the pro-slavery interest had, at the very least, to regard abolition agitation as untimely and impolitic. Pained by the requirements of the planter-farmer-labor bloc, Brownson uttered the *cri de coeur* of a man who represses his instinct for justice in the name of political calculation:

> There is something exceedingly unpleasant in being, even in appearance, opposed to the advocates of freedom. . . . Our own love of excitement, of new things, to say nothing of certain dreams we indulge concerning a golden age that is to be, strongly dispose us to join with the abolitionists, and to rush on in the career they open up to a bold and energetic spirit. There is something, too, in the very idea of freeing two or three millions of slaves, which, in these mechanical and money-getting times is quite refreshing and capable of dazzling the imagination. . . . There is something almost intoxicating in going forth as a bold knight in the cause of humanity, to plead for the wronged and the outraged, to speak for the dumb, and and to do battle for the weak and defenseless.[30]

It was what Brownson thought to be a necessary alliance with the planters which kept him out of the "refreshing," "dazzling," "almost intoxicating" antislavery movement. He resisted the abolitionists out of loyalty to the northern wage workers who, he was convinced, could make no headway against their employers without the powerful aid of the planters. Allying himself with the planters, the enemies of labor's enemies, he attacked the abolitionists vehemently and, in attacking them, sensed he was denying his own deepest inclinations. He consoled himself with the reflection that self-denial was "one of the first laws of morality."[31] Much later he rued the practicality of his politics. "Perhaps," he wrote of the abolitionists during the Civil War, "if we who have so long sneered at them as fanatics, had studied less to be wise and politic, and had been more living men . . . more truly heroic . . . instead of merely prudent and expedient, their fanaticism would have revolted us less."[32]

But during the period of his labor radicalism, Brownson found relief from his qualms about his response to the abolitionists in cataloguing them among the enemies of American liberty:

> The money power is seeking to bind the nation's free spirit with chains of gold, and mistaken philanthropy is fast rending it in twain; associations, sectarian and moral espionage are fast swallowing up individual freedom, and making the individual man but a mere appendage to a huge social machine.[33]

In the American republic, as here represented, capitalists were strengthening the centralist and authoritarian trend in the government and the economy while the abolitionists were trying to tear the Union apart, and Fourierist, temperance, health-food, Sabbath, and other reformers devoured personal freedom. Missing from the catalogue of evildoers is the slave owner, for this is a radical Jacksonian's account of the menaces besetting American liberty. Fixing this aberrant image of America's social ills in his mind, Brownson tried for a time to avoid the dilemma which the coexistence of the wage system and slavery posed for his generation of radicals. But finally, in "The Laboring Classes," the greatest of his radical essays, Brownson faced the political question in the rivalry of two systems of exploitation.

It is better to be a wage worker than a slave, Brownson acknowledged, because the wage worker's "rights as a man are legally recognized, though not in fact enjoyed; for he is nearer the day of his complete enfranchisement, and has greater moral force and more instruments with which to effect it." If it were not for the fact that it is an easier condition from which to escape than chattel slavery, and if Americans had no alternative to the two systems, he would give "preference to the slave system over that of labor at wages."[34] The "pro-slavery" anti-capitalism of Brownson is close to the view expressed by Friedrich Engels in his *Condition of the Workingclass in England*. Writing in 1844, young Engels saw the proletarian "placed in the most revolting, inhuman position conceivable for a human being. The slave is assured of a bare livelihood, the serf has at least a scrap of land on which to live; each has at worst a guarantee for life itself. But the proletarian must depend on himself alone."[35] His intense reaction to the heinousness of capitalism and the misery of the proletariat might have led Engels, as it did Brownson in America and Lassalle in Germany, to seek allies for the workers among the landed opponents of the business community. But the labor radicalism of the Marxists, unlike the varieties associated with Brownson and Lassalle, developed a conditionally positive attitude toward the bourgeoisie and eschewed alliances with junkers and plantation owners. For the sake of the future, the Marxists were willing to support the present against the past; not so Brownson. He would accept neither the capitalist present nor the feudalist past, even provisionally. "We . . . oppose with all our might both systems," he thundered. "We would have neither slave nor proletary."[36] That was his wish; his practice was to support the Democrats.

That practice was a cause of the growing tension between labor radicalism and abolitionism. Among American radicals only Albert Brisbane, Charles Fourier's apostle to the new world, saw a possible way to bring the laborites and the antislavery people together. "It would be a noble step, it strikes me," Brisbane suggested in 1845,

> if the advance guard of the Abolitionists would include in their movement a reform of the present wretched organization of labor, called the wage system. It would add to their power by interesting the producing classes . . . and would prepare a better state for the slaves when emancipated, than the servitude to capital, to which they now seem destined.[37]

But Brownson's hostility to the abolitionists, and the usual indifference of antislavery men to the plight of the wage workers, kept the movement which aimed to revolutionize the South at odds with the one which aimed to revolutionize the North. "Why is it," Brownson asked, "that so few of the real workingmen here are abolitionists?" He himself answered the question, and in answering it disclosed a fatal weakness of the labor radicalism of his time: "It is because they feel that they themselves are virtually slaves, while mocked with the name of freeman, and that the movements in behalf of freedom should best be directed towards their emancipation."[38]

Though bitter and narrow, this answer of Brownson's had some reason in it. As Brownson saw it, social change in the United States would proceed region by region, not nationally. The labor radicals, he believed, could make a social revolution against capital in the North while chattel slavery remained intact in the South. In effect, this was a theory of socialism in one region based on the "law" of uneven development. Moving from the premise that social change occurs at even tempos in all regions (albeit from different starting points), he observed that wage workers are closer to genuine freedom than slaves, and he concluded that the wage workers would achieve freedom before the slaves. This was not a bad syllogism, although it overlooked the possibility that the existence of slavery might arrest the progress of the wage workers and that the slaves might have to win legal emancipation before the wage workers could arrive at "complete enfranchisement."

Brownson's theory of regional revolution was an integral part of his labor radical politics. In developing it, he explored the significance of the American states' rights doctrine for his policy of allying the workers, farmers, and planters. Brownson saw that the national Democratic party was a combination of democrats and anti-democrats and that its make-up prevented its becoming an agency of social change. Nationally, the Democratic party would tend to be neutral on great social issues; only on the state or regional level could it have a coherent social policy. Making a virtue out of this reality, Brownson argued that the federal government ought to be neutral on social issues. With the Democrats at the helm, the federal government would be neutral, but when the Whigs were in power, the federal authority would be used exclusively in the interests of the capitalists. It was therefore in the interest of the labor radicals to keep the Democrats in power in Washington; only then could a labor revolution be carried on in the North without the likelihood of federal counter-revolutionary interference.[39]

If it were to work, the Brownson tactic of using the Jacksonians to abet labor-radical ends needed the mutual loyalty of the allies in the national coalition. On one side, the planter would have to uphold strict construction of the Constitution and oppose the economic policies of the business community. On the other, the wage workers would be required to uphold strict construction while opposing abolitionist subversion of the South's peculiar institution. A lapse on the part of either the planters or the workers would wreck the alliance and might provoke retaliation.

Indeed, the partners in the Jacksonian alliance performed with less than perfect loyalty to one another in the presidential election of 1840. Van Buren and the Democrats lost to Harrison and the Whigs by a margin of almost 150,000 in a popular vote of almost 2,500,000. The Whigs seduced many Jacksonians with the aid of their hard cider and log cabin demagogy, and the result jolted Brownson's faith in the readiness of the working class for enlightened political action. Discouraged by the "maddened and maddening hurrahs of the drunken mob which went for 'Tippecanoe and Tyler too,' "[40] Brownson nevertheless thought that workers who voted for Harrison had not meant to repudiate the Jacksonian program but only to express loss of confidence in the men who had administered it. He was sure that if the Whigs in power attempted to undo the accomplishments of the Jacksonians, the workers would turn the Whigs out at the next election.[41] But Brownson took a far sterner view of southern disloyalty to the Jacksonian alliance. He found no excuses for the planters who had voted Whig, and he threatened the South with the specter of a labor-abolitionist alliance:

> If you desert us, if you side with the business population of the other sections of the country, and aid them in establishing a National Bank, in laying a protective tariff, and assuming directly or indirectly the State Debts, . . . you may rest assured that the Democracy in one solid phalanx will go against your institutions. . . . They feel that you have been neither true to them, nor to yourselves . . . and unless you go *en masse* for the Constitution, you must not be surprised if they go *en masse* against slavery.[42]

Brownson himself was not quick to back up this threat. He did go against slavery in the Civil War, but his immediate response to the collapse of his hope that the Jacksonians would create the opportunity for a labor revolution in the North was to abandon labor radicalism. The American scene was characterized for him by a hateful capitalism, an easily cajoled, helpless working class, and a conservative agrarian South which now appeared to be the only serious counter-force to capitalism. As the conservative and constitutionalist elements in Brownson's political thought came to the fore, he abandoned religious liberalism and sought sanction for his new politics in the Catholic church. "I became henceforth a conservative in politics," he later explained, "instead of an impractical radical, and through political conservation I advanced rapidly toward religious conservatism."[43]

What happened to Brownson thereafter has little relevance for the development of Marxism in America, except for his response to secession and the Civil War. There is a curious parallel, as well as a contrast, between Brownson's response to the Civil War and Marx's. Brownson, a Calhoun supporter at the beginning of his conservative period in 1844, was for Lincoln in the 1860 presidential campaign. In the first year of the war he began to urge immediate emancipation as a means to victory over the Confederacy. Deeming Lincoln's conduct of the war lacking in energy, Brownson supported the radical John C. Frémont for the Republican nomination in 1864.[44] If this looks like capricious behavior in an old admirer of Calhoun and a professed enemy of social radicalism, it is not. Brownson's militant support of the North during the Civil War was calculated to make the United States safe for conservatism. In his radical period Brownson had seen the southern slave-holders as a force which could keep the northern capitalists from using the federal power for their own ends and so provide opportunity for a labor revolution in the North.

Having himself become a conservative, Brownson now saw that the South's rulers might play an entirely different role in national politics. It now appeared to him that the South ought to be kept in the Union to weigh against northern radicalism, not for it. If, as Brownson expected, no radical reconstruction of southern society took place after the defeat of the Confederacy, the South would exercise a conservative influence on the nation. As early as 1865 he spelled out this prediction of the trend of American politics in *The American Republic:*

> In the states that seceded socialism has never had a foothold, and will not gain it, for it is resisted by all the sentiments, convictions, and habits of the southern people, and the southern people will not be exterminated nor swamped by migrations from the North or from Europe. They are and always will be an agricultural people, and agricultural people are and always will be opposed to socialistic dreams, unless unwittingly led for a moment to favor it. . . .

He denounced the idea of "hanging, exiling, or disfranchising the wealthy landholders of the South, in order to bring up the poor and depressed whites," but was sure that "that policy will never be carried out." As for the Negroes, if "enfranchised, they will always vote with the wealthy landholding class, and aid them in resisting socialistic tendencies."[45] In 1865 Brownson was the prophet of the Dixiecrat coalition which was to endure for generations as a bulwark against leftward change in America.

Marx, of course, was also a supporter of the Union in the Civil War, but for different reasons than Brownson. Like Brownson, he was sometimes critical of what seemed to him Lincoln's indecisiveness. In arguing the case for speedy emancipation, Marx even quoted Brownson, but he did not go to Brownson's extreme of advocating the replacement of Lincoln by Frémont in 1864.[46] Marx hoped that destruction of the slave system through victory for the Union would bring the American people to grips with the labor question. "Every independent movement of the workers was paralyzed so long as slavery disfigured part of the Republic," he wrote in *Capital* in 1867, and he implied that an aftermath of the war would be the rise of a strong American labor movement which could make capitalism versus socialism a practical issue in the United States.[47] The crisis of secession and reunion, however, was resolved in a manner more to Brownson's liking than to Marx's. Twelve years after the war the party of northern business made a deal with the party of southern planters.

The Compromise of 1877, which gave Hayes the Presidency

and the white supremacists the South, "scotched," in the words of C. Vann Woodward, "any tendency of the South to combine forces with the internal enemies of the new economy—laborites, Western agrarians, reformers."[48] It also generally confirmed for a long time the vision of Brownson and disappointed the vision of Marx. There are times in history when brilliant cynicism provides a clearer outlook on the future than does generous hope. Marx knew that there could be no socialism in the United States without the fraternal unity of black and white workers, that "labour cannot emancipate itself in the white skin where in the black it is branded," but in 1867 he mistakenly assumed that the brand was removed from the blacks, that the Civil War had truly freed the Negro.[49] Even before it ended Brownson had a clearer idea of what the Civil War might accomplish. "You will never," he told the abolitionists in the third year of the war, "make the mass of the white people look upon the blacks as their equals." And he understood that race prejudice would bolster the conservative principle of hierarchy in American society. "We talk no more of elevating the laboring classes," said this ex-radical. "All cannot stand at the top of society, for if all were at the top there would be no bottom and society would be the bottomless pit."[50] However he felt little need to worry about the possibility of the triumph of hellish social equality in America. Brownson knew that abolition would encourage attempts to gain full equality for the Negro, to establish the rights of women, and to abolish private property. But egalitarian radicals, he predicted, would not advance far along the road to socialism in America. He cheerfully affirmed in 1865 that with the abolition of slavery, "there is no social grievance of magnitude enough to enlist any considerable number of people . . . in a movement to redress it." He recalled that the abolitionists "could not and never did carry the nation, even in the question of slavery itself" before the war. Now, after the war, "the exclusion of negro suffrage can never be made to appear to the American people as anything like so great a grievance as was slavery."[51] It was to be a long time before this analysis would begin to be outdated.

It is small wonder that the energies of Brownson and his generation of American radicals were expended at cross-purposes.

Class struggle in America before the Civil War could not develop along simple capital-versus-labor lines. The complexities of inter-class alliances and antagonisms made it hard for the radicals to know what to do next; they consequently had many causes but no unifying cause. Brownson had tried to change the situation by subordinating all other radical causes to that of the wage workers. It had seemed reasonable to him not to try to attack all injustices simultaneously, and to ask the slaves and the women to give precedence to the workers. The antislavery men and the feminists never saw the point. "The genuine Yankee," Brownson once com-plained, "is never satisfied with doing one thing at a time. He is really in his glory only when he has a dozen or more irons in the fire at once."[52] Trying to avoid what struck him as the futile multi-fariousness of Yankee radical activity, Brownson became a proto-type of the American labor radical. Scouting abolition and ignor-ing other non-labor reform movements, Brownson, on joining the Jacksonians, found himself compelled to center his attention on issues—such as banking—having little bearing on the largest issue to face his generation: the slavery question. Abolitionists and other radicals tended to respond in kind with indifference or hos-tility to the cause of labor.

After the war a new selection of labor radicals appeared. Older men like Wendell Phillips, Stephen Pearl Andrews, and William West were links between the old radicalism and the new. But the continuity they supplied was too thin to naturalize the alien radicalism of the Germans who shaped socialism in America between the Civil War and the rise of the De Leon and Debs movements. Brownson himself symbolizes the discontinuity be-tween the first American labor radicals and their successors. His radicalism perished from a dilemma he could not grapple with, avoid, or wish out of existence.

### HERMAN KRIEGE

A twenty-five year old German arrived in New York in September 1845 and promptly took up the cause of American labor radicalism which Brownson had recently abandoned; he was

Herman Kriege.[53] In Germany he had been a member of the circle of communists associated with Marx. When Kriege began to publish his German-language labor paper *Volkstribun* in January 1846, he emerged as probably the world's first former Marxist and certainly as the first refugee from Marxism to arrive in America. Kriege was a total convert to the Brownsonian variety of labor radicalism, and his quarrel with Marx, which he aired in the *Volkstribun,* foreshadowed later controversies between Marxists and representatives of indigenous American radicalism.

When Kriege's *Volkstribun* reached Europe Marx and his circle were in Brussels, exiles from the Prussian Rhineland. What they read in the paper nettled the Marxists. Kriege was quickly falling under the spell of the American agrarian faith. In the tenth number of the *Volkstribun,* for example, Kriege celebrated the United States as the land of dreams come true. Here, he said, the peasants of Europe have "an abode which they have only to occupy and bring to fruitfulness with the labor of their hands before calling out proudly and defiantly to all the tyrants of the world: 'Das ist meine Huette,/Die ihr nicht gebaut,/Das ist mein Herd/ Um dessen Glut ihr mich beneidet.' " This picture of a husbandman glorying in possession of his cabin and taunting an overlord who envies the warmth of his hearth, brought the jeering suggestion from the brash young men in Brussels that Kriege ought to add another stanza to the poem to praise the husbandman's dunghill. This Marxist hostility to agrarianism recalls the disaffection of two Americans who gave the agrarian dream the same connotation at about the same time. "It is my opinion," Hawthorne wrote in his notebook while at Brook Farm, "that a man's soul may be buried and perish under a dung-heap, or in the furrow of the field, just as well as under a pile of money."[54] And Thoreau lashed out in *Walden* at the model farm "where the house stands like a fungus in a muck-heap . . . Stocked with men! A great grease-spot, redolent of manures and buttermilk! Under a high state of cultivation, being manured with the hearts and brains of men!"

But Kriege saw the American farm as a social panacea. He claimed, in the thirteenth number of his paper, that distribution of 55,000 acres of land on Long Island would stamp out crime and pauperism in New York City for all eternity. Marx and his friends called this "economic naiveté." Even on the broad scale of the North American continent, they argued, free soil would not be an everlasting cure-all for American social ills. "If the population of the United States grows at the same rate as up till now (that is, if it doubles every twenty-five years), this 'all eternity' will not last forty years. And since free distribution of land will vastly increase immigration, Kriege's 'eternity' will be gone all the sooner."

Not Kriege's support for the free-soil idea but the unqualifiedness of that support bothered the Marxists:

> Had Kriege adhered to the free-soil movement as a first form of the proletarian movement, necessary under the given conditions but necessarily developing towards communism because of the social position of the class initiating it, had he shown that the trend toward communism in America must emerge from this agrarianism which is seemingly contradictory to all communism, there would have been nothing to say against it.

They spoke against it because Kriege had accepted the American farmer as the agent who would realize the good society. Kriege indeed was forthrightly claiming a messianic role for the overwhelmingly rural American masses. He called "the majority of this people our savior." He "resolved to appeal to its judgment and repose all wishes and hopes for mankind in its solicitude." He thought it was the only people "fitted to take the good society out of the blue sky and put it on the solid earth." He had therefore flung himself into American politics, specifically into Democratic politics, as "the only means to work effectively against the despotism of capital." In following this course he was "untroubled by the grimaces of sneering philosophers."

The philosophers of Brussels in turn denounced "the fantastic rhapsody which Kriege preaches under the name of communism in New York." Kriege's propaganda of agrarian utopianism, they felt, could arrest the growth of working-class élan if the workers accepted it. He was not preparing the workers for militant class struggle. "It amounts to sentimental drivel," they complained, "when

Kriege represents communism as the benevolent antithesis of egoism and reduces a world-historical revolutionary movement to the
paired words Love-Hate, Communism-Egoism." While nascent
Marxism in 1846 was ridding itself of the gentle language of ethical
reform which had characterized the utopian socialists and was
acquiring the ferocious vocabulary of class struggle, Kriege was
continuing in America to speak of communism in terms which
resembled those of Emerson who had expressed his hope (in "Politics") "that thousands of human beings might exercise towards each
other the grandest and simplest sentiments, as well as a knot of
friends, or a pair of lovers."

Kriege naturally did not use the language of love in his po-
lemic against the Marxists. Under the caption "A Bull of Anathema," he did them the courtesy of publishing their criticism of
his American politics in the twenty-third and twenty-fourth
numbers of the *Volkstribun*. In his reply to the Marxists, Kriege
took the stance of a busy, practical American telling off the idle
theorists of Europe. He had had enough of their passivity even
before he left Europe, having realized that "enduring prosperity,
peace, and freedom can prevail nowhere in the world until the
frightful split between work and enjoyment, poverty and riches,
is abolished in fact, not merely criticized." He was tired of the
accumulation of useless knowledge. "Should we, like precocious
schoolboys, make wise remarks about things everybody knows,
which help not even a single individual? Having renounced such
exercises body and soul, did we escape from critical Europe only
to take them up once again?" Kriege was perhaps reminding Marx
of his aphorism about the need to change the world. "The question was 'What shall we do?' If the critical gentlemen of Brussels
had been with us at the time, they would probably have repudiated this first question as 'uncommunist' since the word 'do' is
not, as you know, to be found in the lexicon of the critic."

Kriege was convinced that he spoke for an active American
alternative to the theoretical communism of Europe. He shared
Brownson's faith that the United States "is the country in which
the noble ideas of man and society, which French and German
scholars strike out in their speculations, are first to be applied to

practice, realized in institutions." Emboldened by that faith, Kriege baited the Marxists. "Where," he inquired, "do the gentlemen of Brussels think to begin the work [of changing the world]? Must they not be uneasy to descend from their critical heights and make a beginning somewhere? Now then, where will they make this beginning? In England? France? Germany? Might they not tell us what they are doing to revolutionize the proletariat over there?" The Revolution of 1848 was soon to give "the critical gentlemen" an opportunity to go from study to action in Germany, but to Kriege in 1846 they appeared to be permanently immobilized. "The business of Mssrs. Marx, Engels, and so forth," he concluded,

> is the critical description of the communist movement, the description of the family, marriage, and so forth. All these things interest them no further than as subject matter for description. And they imagine that I have nothing better to do here in America than to make critical glosses on the given conditions and that the *Volkstribun* has no other purpose than to describe the forthcoming movement.

As a labor radical immersed in the politics of his time, Kriege of course had to declare his stand on abolition; the stand he took was Brownsonian. "The slavery question," he wrote in the *Volkstribun* (November 21, 1846), "cannot be separately resolved." Under existing conditions abolition would "thrust our republic into anarchy, increase the monstrous competition among the 'free workers' and debase labor itself. . . . we will not better the position of our 'black brothers' through abolition but will infinitely worsen the condition of our 'white brothers.'" His prescription for the slaves was gradualism. "We believe in the peaceful evolution of society in the United States. . . . For this reason we remain pledged to work against abolition with all our might, despite all the entreaties of sentimental philistines and all the poesy of lady enthusiasts for freedom." Like Brownson before him, Kriege was caught in the dilemma of American radicals in the 1840's; but not for long. He returned to Germany during the Revolution. After its defeat, he fled to the United States, and at his death in 1851 was a minor figure in the Tammany organization.

**Orestes Brownson**

Joseph Weydemeyer in Union Army.

Friedrich A. Sorge and his wife.

# Chapter 3

# The German-American Marxists:
# Weydemeyer and Sorge

## JOSEPH WEYDEMEYER

Among the young Germans in Brussels who discussed and denounced Kriege's American politics in 1846 was Joseph Weydemeyer. The controversy was probably of more lasting significance to him than to the others because it was a foretaste of the difficulties of Marxism in America which he himself would meet at close range in the 1850's and 1860's.

Born in 1818, the same year as Marx, Weydemeyer was the son of a Prussian civil servant residing in Muenster in Westphalia.[1] To prepare him for the army, Weydemeyer was sent to a gymnasium and the Berlin military academy; in 1838 he received his commission. In his early twenties, Weydemeyer was stationed in the Westphalian town of Minden. There he began to read and respond to the bourgeois radical and socialistic ideas of the *Rheinische Zeitung*, the Cologne paper Marx became editor of before the Prussian censorship suppressed it in 1843. This paper was a harbinger of the revolution of 1848. It undermined the allegiance to the Hohenzollern monarchy of many soldiers garrisoned in the Rhineland and Westphalia. In the Minden garrison alone the paper helped make revolutionaries out of Fritz Anneke, August Willich, Hermann Korff, and Friedrich von Buest—all of whom, like Weydemeyer, were to become prominent forty-eighters and subsequently officers of the Union army in the Civil War. The leftist officers in Minden formed a study circle in which Weydemeyer took part. He also went frequently to Cologne to attend discussions of social problems which the journalists of the *Rheinische Zeitung* conducted. In 1844 Weydemeyer resigned from the Prussian Army. He was committed to socialism by then and must have sensed that, in Prussia at any rate, an army career was incompatible with effective expression of his new views. (In America, by contrast, he would find it possible to be both a Marxist propagandist and an army officer.)

On doffing his uniform in 1844, Weydemeyer became assistant editor of the *Trierische Zeitung,* a paper which advocated the Phalansteries of Charles Fourier and the True Socialism of Karl Gruen. The next year Weydemeyer joined the *Westphaelische Dampfboot* after paying a visit to Marx, exiled in Paris. Marx, and Engels as well, were publishing in the *Dampfboot* at the time. The paper was edited by Otto Luening in Bielefeld and Paderborn. (Luening's sister Luise became Weydemeyer's wife in 1845.)

After a second visit to Marx (Brussels, 1846), Weydemeyer went back to Germany to take a hand in organizing the Communist League in Cologne. This was the organization Marx and Engels wrote the *Communist Manifesto* for in 1847. While organizing for the league, Weydemeyer continued to work on the *Dampfboot.* Meanwhile, he made his living as a construction engineer for the Cologne-Minden Railroad, but he quit the job soon after the outbreak of the revolution in 1848 because the railroad ordered its employees to stay out of political demonstrations.

During the rest of 1848, and for more than a year thereafter, Weydemeyer was a full-time revolutionary journalist. He was invited to Darmstadt (in June 1848) by the socialist publisher C. W. Leske to be co-editor with Otto Luening of the *Neue Deutsche*

*Zeitung.* Darmstadt is near Frankfurt where the German National Assembly was meeting in 1848, and the socialist brothers-in-law sought to make their new paper a channel of communication between the left wing of the Assembly and the extra-parliamentary movement. In 1849 the triumphant counter-revolution cut short this effort. Prussian absolutism swept away the Frankfurt Assembly, crushed the armed democracy in Baden and the Palatinate, and suppressed all the pro-democratic papers it could reach. Marx's *Neue Rheinische Zeitung* was closed down, but the *Neue Deûtsche Zeitung* escaped for a while by moving from Darmstadt to Frankfurt in the spring of 1849. There Weydemeyer kept it coming out in the face of increasingly stringent censorship until December 1850 when the senate of that imperial free city banished its editors. Ejected from Frankfurt, Weydemeyer remained in Germany for half a year, underground. With the Prussian police on his trail he fled to Switzerland (July 1851) with his wife and two children. In Switzerland Weydemeyer could not find a job. He wrote to Marx from Zurich on July 27 that he saw no alternative to migrating to the United States. Like other forty-eighters he accepted reluctantly the idea of going to America; it would be a place of temporary exile, he hoped.

In his response to Weydemeyer's letter, Marx recommended that he settle in New York. Marx thought New York was the most likely place to bring out a new German-language revolutionary journal to fill the void created by the abrogation of press freedom in Germany. It was "not far removed from Europe," and New York was the American city in which Europeans might best insulate themselves from the call of the wild. "Once across the ocean," fretted Marx, "who will guarantee that you will not lose yourself somewhere in the Far West? We have so few forces, we must be so sparing with our talents." Engels, who was in on the discussion of Weydemeyer's plans, tried to reassure Marx. "After all," he observed, "New York is not out of the world."[2] Then he gave Weydemeyer a sharp vignette of the American scene: "Your greatest handicap will be the fact that useful Germans who are worth anything are easily Americanized and abandon all hope of returning home." He went on to remark "the special American conditions" which could be expected to limit the appeal of socialism in the United States: "the ease with which the surplus population is drained off to the farms, the necessarily rapid and rapidly growing prosperity of the country, which makes bourgeois conditions look like a *beau ideal*" to Americans.[3]

Weydemeyer and his family sailed from Le Havre on September 29, 1851 and arrived in New York on November 7. His American career will be traced after a consideration of the German background of Friedrich Sorge who, after Weydemeyer, was the principal exponent of Marxism in the United States until Daniel De Leon took command of the Socialist Labor party in the 1890's.[4]

Ten years younger than Weydemeyer, Friedrich Albert Sorge was born November 29, 1828 in his father's parsonage at Bethau, near Torgau in Saxony. Though a member of the established Lutheran Church, Parson Sorge was a child of the Enlightenment at heart. He was the kind of clergyman who in the New England of his day was abandoning Calvinist orthodoxy in favor of unitarianism, and who was attracted to abolition and other reform movements. In the era of Metternich, in Prussianized Saxony, the liberal impulse of the elder Sorge found an outlet in the Polish national-liberation struggle. He put his parsonage at the disposal of the Polish revolutionaries. It served them as a station on the underground railway along which they shuttled between Poland, France, and Belgium. Emissaries of Polish revolutionary circles in exile would lodge in the Sorge household and then travel twenty-five or thirty miles to the next station on the underground. Friedrich was aware from early childhood that his father was sheltering refugees from autocracy; one of them became Friedrich's boyhood hero. He was Robert Blum, a plebian democrat who aided the Polish uprising of 1831 and died before a Hapsburg firing squad in 1849.

The Sorge family was large and poor. The parson taught his children himself. He instructed Friedrich in Latin, Greek, history, and literature until the boy was ready for the free seminary in Halle. Friedrich went to Halle, but historic events put an end to his formal education. The seminary proved not to be the route to a parsonage of his own but to a footing on the barricades.

Sorge was nineteen when the revolution of 1848 broke out, and his role in the tragic German contest between liberal-democratic nationalism and feudal-bureaucratic nationalism was naturally less prominent than that of Weydemeyer who was ten years his senior. Sorge joined a band of armed revolutionaries in Saxony that was promptly squelched by counter-revolutionary troops from Pomerania. In the spring of 1849 Sorge went to Switzerland and waited for a chance to intervene again in the struggle in Germany. He had not waited long when news reached him that the Badenese army had revolted and forced the Grand Duke of Baden to flee his duchy. Sorge thereupon crossed into Germany and hastened toward Karlsruhe, the capital of Baden. He was in company with August Willich, a comrade of Weydemeyer's from the Minden garrison, who was destined to become a Union general in the Civil War. With Willich, Sorge joined the *Karlsruhe Freikorps* and fought against the Prussians in various battles in Baden and Palatinate. Friedrich Engels, another participant in this campaign, served as *aide-de-camp* to Willich. It is likely that in this campaign, in which German democracy made its last stand against Prussian autocracy, Sorge and Engels first met, but possibly they did not meet until later in 1849 when both of them were refugees in Geneva and in touch with Wilhelm Liebknecht.[5]

When the Prussian army had routed the armed revolutionaries in Baden and the Palatinate, the latter crossed the Swiss frontier and were disarmed. Along with other survivors of the defeated force, Sorge was interned in Freiburg but later permitted to go to Geneva where he arrived in September 1849. Unlike Weydemeyer who had a wife and two children to support, Sorge, a single youth of twenty, was able to maintain himself in Switzerland. Drawing upon the cultural heritage of a Lutheran parsonage, he found a livelihood as a music teacher. In Geneva Sorge joined Liebknecht's Workers' Cultural Society and got to know such German leftists as the True Socialist, Moses Hess; the Marxist, Johann Phillip Becker; and Fritz Kaum and Fritz Jacoby, two men of undefined radical bent whom he would meet again in New York German circles during the 1850's. He also consorted with a group of juvenile exiles who called themselves the *Schwefelbunde;* these brimstone boys found unpolitical and impolitic ways of annoying stolid Geneva citizens, the Swiss government, and the police. In the summer of 1851, when he had been in Switzerland almost two years, the police told Sorge to get out of the country. Expelled from Switzerland, Sorge went to Liège in Belgium where a brother of his was living. He worked in Liège in a carpenter shop and subsequently was a teacher of German in a private school. Meanwhile, the Belgian police kept him under surveillance, ordering his expulsion (in March 1852) after a stay of only about half a year. His choice of countries of refuge was steadily narrowing. France, under the dictatorship of Napoleon III, was out of the question. He could not return to Germany for a court-martial at Torgau had condemned him, in absentia, to death because of his part in the revolution. So Sorge crossed to England and looked for work, without success, in London. It seemed that he would have to leave Europe.

Before quitting London Sorge called on Marx. Their conversation at this first meeting was perfunctory, for Marx seems to have regarded his young visitor less as a comrade than as an interruption.[6] Indeed, Sorge in 1852 was not close to Marx in outlook. He was, in fact, in that wing of 1848 radicalism, more bourgeois than laborite, which did not share Marx's concern for the conditions and destiny of the workers, and which centered its thinking on the enlightenment of humanity rather than on the emancipation of a class. Marx could have had no inkling that Sorge would develop, in the American environment, into his mainstay there. He could not even have known that Sorge was on his way to America; Sorge himself did not know it until he was already at sea.

To Sorge, out of work in London, the idea of settling in the United States was repugnant. Regarding this country as a land of slave-drivers and slave-catchers, he preferred to go to Australia. Before he could act, this inexperienced young German, who spoke no English, came down with cholera. While still weak and dazed with illness, he was set aboard the Independence a few hours before it left for New York. After a voyage he had not intended, Sorge landed in what seemed the wrong country. He arrived in New York on June 21, 1852. There he found Weydemeyer already deeply involved in propagandizing and organizing for the Marxist cause.

## WEYDEMEYER IN AMERICA

Within a month of his landing at New York Weydemeyer (in December 1851) issued a prospectus for a paper he wished to bring out named *Die Revolution*. "It will be the task of the new weekly," he announced, "to give as clear a picture of the class struggle which is becoming ever more concentrated in the Old World and can only end in the abolition of all class differences."[7] He next acquired the names of four hundred subscribers to an expiring New York German periodical, and advertised in the New York *Turn-Zeitung* of New Year's Day, 1852, that

> *Die Revolution*, a weekly edited by J. Weydemeyer, former editor of the *Neue Deutsche Zeitung* which was supressed by the police in Frankfort-am-Main, will appear every Sunday with the collaboration of the editors of the former *Neue Rheinische Zeitung*, Karl Marx, Friedrich Engels, Ferdinand Freiligrath, etc.

The paper appeared January 6 but was suspended with the issue of January 13. The response among German immigrants was simply too small to sustain a Marxist weekly in America. Weydemeyer explained the failure of *Die Revolution* to Marx when he wrote him at the end of January:

> For some time now the workers here have been exploited in so many various ways. First Kinkel, then Kossuth, and most of them are assinine enough to contribute a dollar for this hostile propaganda rather than a penny for the expression of their own interests. The American soil has a most corrupting effect on people and at the same time fills them with arrogance, as if they were far superior to their comrades in the Old World.[8]

The exasperated Weydemeyer put his difficulties in proper perspective when he placed his competitive relationship to the liberal bourgeois nationalists in the foreground. The outpouring of immigrant dollars to liberal knights-errant like Professor Gottfried Kinkel—whom Carl Shurz had recently helped to escape from a German prison—and Louis Kossuth, the lionized leader of the Hungarian revolution, understandably vexed Weydemeyer. Those dollars flowed more readily to the liberals than immigrant pennies trickled into the till of the Marxist paper. German immigrants were not avid to read Marx's explanations of the triumph of European reaction, or Freiligrath's lampoons of the quixotic posturings of the exiled heroes of 1848. Marxism was most hindered in its first efforts to find a following in the United States because it was not romantic enough. The arrogance shown by Germans acclimated in "the American soil" toward newcomers from the Fatherland was a problem time would rapidly solve for Weydemeyer. But Weydemeyer did not survive long enough for time to solve the problem which exile optimism constituted for him and for Marxism in America.

Weydemeyer brought out Marx's *Eighteenth Brumaire of Louis Bonaparte* as a final number of *Die Revolution* (spring 1852), after arranging for serial publication of Engels' *Peasant War in Germany* in the New York *Turn-Zeitung* (January 1852–February 1853). Meanwhile, Weydemeyer himself was writing frequently for the Turner paper. His contributions reveal a man initially preoccupied with refugee politics but who developed a concern for large political issues which drew him out of the circle of frustrated exiles.

His very first article for the *Turn-Zeitung* (January 1, 1852) attempted to set at rest American aversion to the Marxist idea of proletarian dictatorship. "The rule of the proletariat," he insists, "has nothing in common with brutal vandalism: on the contrary, the proletariat is the only class in a position to carry forward the entire heritage of the bourgeoisie." His next articles attacked a liberal refugee group which was calling for free elections in Europe but saying nothing about the conditions of the workers. The right to vote, argued Weydemeyer, is not a panacea, since

in bourgeois society the basis of universal suffrage lies in the economic dependence of the voter, which often forces the worker, for the sake of his own existence, to sell his vote to capital and keeps the rural population in a backward condition, the inevitable consequence of their isolation and chronic poverty.[9]

Weydemeyer's next target was the efforts of forty-eighters to raise money in the United States to foment revolution in Europe. The success of such efforts, he thought, only revealed the political immaturity of those who supported them.

> Revolutions are not "made"; on the contrary, they are brought about by the appearance of circumstances over which individuals have no control. Indeed, it would be sad for the peoples of Europe if their fate could be decided by collecting a few paltry dollars.[10]

Having written a series of articles which counterposed Marxism to liberalism for the German immigrants, Weydemeyer began (in the July number of the *Turn-Zeitung*) discussion of labor issues in the United States; free trade versus protection was the first issue he looked at. As a Marxist, Weydemeyer favored industrial development and recognized the role tariffs played in promoting it. But he was in no hurry to commit himself on the trade controversy. The American working class, he thought, would be wise to remain unpledged either to free trade or protective tariffs until it had more time to judge how alternative policies would affect its standard of living.

Turning to the central question of American politics of the fifties, Weydemeyer (in the *Turn-Zeitung* of September 1) analyzed the relationship between "Australian Cotton and American Slavery." The passing of the American monopoly on the world market, he speculated, promoted the rise of truly national parties in American politics and a national rather than regional development of the industrial economy:

> . . . the sectional tendencies of the South, its special interests, are no longer valid: the parties will develop more sharply and clearly defined over the whole country. The American feeling of independence, which imagines that Americans are less subject to the influence of industrialization than the peoples of old Europe, is over and done with. And so is the cherished supremacy of the agricultural over the industrial interests . . . .

Weydemeyer had the Marxist gift for discerning fundamental historical trends, and the Marxist weakness for greatly fore-shortening the development of those trends.

Weydemeyer concluded his first year's journalistic work with a review of the election campaign of 1852, noting (in the *Turn-Zeitung* of November 15) the absence of labor planks in the platforms of the Whig and Democratic parties. There followed in the December issues of the paper a two-part "Political-Economic Survey." This essay was Weydemeyer's first attempt to project a platform for American labor. In it he argued the case for organization of the workers on a large scale along political and economic lines, and urged the workers to adopt an internationalist outlook based on recognition of the interdependence of political and economic conditions in this country and Europe.

With four of his friends, Weydemeyer formed the first Marxist organization in the United States in the summer of 1852.[11] The *Proletarierbund*, as this tiny group was called, won the attention of a surprising number of German immigrants. On its initiative, eight hundred German Americans assembled in Mechanics' Hall in New York City on March 20, 1853 to found the American Workers League. This new venture was a quasi-party, quasi-trade-union organization and was typical of workers' movements of the period in the old world and the new. Its Marxist leaders drafted a program designed to gain access to the non-socialist bulk of the working class by emphasizing issues of immediate relevance in the United States, without losing sight of the socialist goal.

The program declared for immediate naturalization of all immigrants who legally signified their intentions to become American citizens. Departing from the tradition of American labor radicalism represented by Brownson, it favored federal, rather than state, labor legislation. Its legislative planks included guaranteed payment of wages to workers whose employers went bankrupt, and assumption by government of all costs of litigation with free choice of counsel—to keep the affluent from monopolizing the best lawyers. It was for reducing the working day, traditionally the sunlight hours, to ten hours. It was for banning labor for children under sixteen, and for compulsory education with government maintenance for children whose families were too poor to provide it. (This was a modification of the state boarding-school proposal of the Robert Dale Owen wing of the Workingmen's party.) Showing the Teutonic and rationalist heritage of its authors, the program came out against all Sunday and temperance laws. The program called for the formation of tuition-free colleges and for state acquisition of existing private colleges. Finally, it sought to keep the national lands on the frontier inalienable and urged their cultivation by associations sponsored by the government in the national interest.[12] Of the demands in the program of the American Workers League, only the last mentioned proved to be inapplicable to American conditions, for it flew in the face of the tradition and continuing movement of American free-soil radicalism.

The league's platform of immediate demands was appended to a declaration of revolutionary principles. "So long as industry serves capital alone," declared this preamble, "our situation must worsen every day." The preamble charged the capitalists with responsibility for anti-labor legislation and set for the league the task of organizing "a firmly united and independent political party to assert and realize the rights of the workers." The preamble designated the taking of political power by the working class as the means for resolving all social and political issues. It made the league open to all workers "without respect to occupation, language, color, or sex."

The preamble shows its Marxist authors were attempting to relate their principles to American political tradition. "All parties appeal to the words and proclamations of the Fathers of the Republic, and we now follow their example," it asserted, going on to endorse the self-evident truths of the Declaration of Independence. These truths, however, remain only partly realized. The country has won its political independence, but its citizens have not gained their individual independence.

> America is free from the princely yoke and has no hereditary ranks. But that does not change the fact that the man without property has nothing but his labor power and is oppressed and exploited here as he is on the other side of the ocean. The only difference is that over there the bourgeois is monarchist and over here republican.[13]

The American Workers League functioned for several years in the mid-fifties under a central committee made up of delegates from ward clubs and trade unions. As a member of this committee, Weydemeyer tried to get the league to outgrow its exclusively German character through involvement in American economic and political struggles. The league, however, survived primarily as a German recreation and mutual aid society existing in isolation from the English-speaking workers. It never was able to fill the role of a union central body or a labor party.

In the context of the Know-Nothing agitation of the period, the league's failure to reach out toward the native-born worker and to grapple with American issues was perhaps inescapable. When, in 1855, the members began forming a secret military organization to defend themselves against nativist attacks, Weydemeyer withdrew from the league. Rather than going along with undercover derring-do, he preferred to devote himself, for the time being, to study of the American economy and to writing and lecturing in behalf of Marxist ideas; for, like Marx, Weydemeyer was unsentimental toward foundering organizations.[14] Convinced of the need to organize the working class, he nevertheless recognized, in 1855, that the first effort to imbue an American organization with Marxist principles and tactics had gone awry, and he left the American Workers League to its own devices.

During Weydemeyer's first decade in the United States, the country was moving toward civil war. In the events leading up to the conflict, German Americans played a meaningful part; they were of particular importance in the emergence of the Republican party. Weydemeyer was among the articulate men who drew the German community toward the Republicans and the antislavery cause. In this effort Weydemeyer was working counter to the influence of more prominent labor radicals. Wilhelm Weitling, for instance, showed affinity for the Democrats when he was not manifesting utopian disdain for political involvement of any kind, and he avoided attacks on slavery in his labor paper. William Sylvis, emerging at the end of the decade as the leading native-born trade unionist, was also aloof from the Republicans.[15]

The Germans came over to the Republicans as they learned that slavery—not nativism, temperance, or the clergy in politics—was the cardinal American issue in the fifties. Many Germans who had begun political life in America as Democrats found their way to the Republican party through the free-soil movement. Like all nineteenth-century Marxists, however, Weydemeyer was against parcelling out government lands to small farmers. In the face of swelling support for the Homestead bill in 1854, Weydemeyer favored the "introduction of large-scale agriculture in those vast areas known as state lands," and a linking of industry and agriculture that would make "a healthy life and a healthy home no longer seem incompatible with large-scale business undertakings." It is a credit to Weydemeyer's sense of proportion that he did not let his belief in factories-in-the-fields keep him out of the political movement which brought Lincoln to the presidency. His fear that the Homestead bill would ultimately be detrimental to the interests of the workers did not keep him from seeing that the Republicans were a vehicle for a progressive solution to the slavery question. By 1860 he had shelved his original farm policy and, together with other German Republicans, was urging the Republicans to campaign for "immediate passage by Congress of a Homestead law by which the public lands of the Union may be secured for homesteads of the people, and secured from the greed of speculators."[16]

Weydemeyer's change of position on what to do with the western lands was tactical rather than fundamental. In 1845 Hermann Kriege had rapturously endorsed the free-soil movement in his New York *Volkstribun* and had been attacked for his stand by Marx, Weydemeyer, and other German communists who were then in Brussels. But the Marxists had attacked Kriege not because he supported the movement, but because he regarded it as a social panacea. When fifteen years later Weydemeyer adapted himself to the popular movement for a homestead law, he had not arrived at Kriege's position because he continued thereafter to speak and act from the socialist conviction that something far other than land distribution was required for building the New Jerusalem in the United States. The political context of land reform had changed significantly in fifteen years. In 1860 it was possible to oppose slavery and back the Homestead law at the same time; in 1845, by contrast, the free-soil issue appeared more an alternative than a complement to the antislavery movement, and support for it was likely to be coupled with support for the Democrats. The political travels of Kriege had ended in Tammany Hall;[17] Weydemeyer's ended in the First International. Weydemeyer's tactical shift of position foreshadowed similar shifts imposed on Marxists in other countries where small farmers and would-be small farmers were a strong political influence.[18] Later American Marxists also felt the pressure of the agrarian dream but were, as will be seen, less willing to accommodate themselves to that pressure than Weydemeyer was.

Shortly after dropping out of the American Workers League, Weydemeyer left New York for the midwest where he lived for four years, first in Milwaukee and then in Chicago. He continued his journalism and lecturing and also worked as a surveyor. In Chicago Weydemeyer made another abortive attempt to establish an independent German labor paper, and he contributed to the Illinois *Staatszeitung*, the most influential German Republican daily in the midwest. He also took part in the *Deutsches Haus* conference of German-American societies which met in Chicago in May 1860 to influence the Republican convention's platform and choice of candidates. He was back in New York by early fall of 1860 to take a job as a surveyor of Central Park. In the election campaign he was an active Lincoln man.[19] Eight months later he was in the army.

Because of his background as a Prussian artillery officer and surveyor, Weydemeyer was appointed a technical aide on the staff of General John C. Frémont, the commander of the Department of the West. Under Frémont, Weydemeyer superintended the erection of ten forts around St. Louis. After Frémont was removed from his command in November 1861, Weydemeyer was made a lieutenant colonel and given command of a Missouri volunteer artillery regiment which took the field against Confederate guerillas in southern Missouri in 1862. At the end of the year he was hospitalized for a nervous disorder and transferred to garrison duty in St. Louis where he was mustered out in September 1863.

Weydemeyer was politically active in Missouri for about a year while he was out of uniform. Two political problems were uppermost in his mind at this time: the extension of emancipation to Missouri, and prevention of a split in Missouri between the Lincoln and Frémont factions of the Republican party. His stand on border-state slavery was that of a radical Republican impatient with the policy of conciliating loyalist slave-holders. This was the Frémont position. But though friendly to Fremont, Weydemeyer wished to conciliate the moderate Lincoln men and keep the Republicans intact for the sake of victory in the 1864 election and in the war.[20]

Weydemeyer rejoined the army in September 1864 as colonel of the Forty-first Infantry Missouri Volunteers charged with guarding part of St. Louis and an adjacent area. This was easy work; while doing his military duties he found time to distribute copies of the Inaugural Address of the International Workingmen's Association, exchange letters with Engels on military and political topics, and contribute to the local papers, including the *Daily St. Louis Press* for which he wrote an editorial greeting the founding of the First International. Weydemeyer demobilized his regiment and left the army in July 1865.

Weydemeyer, with the end of the war, began to write regularly for the *Westliche Post* and the *Neue Zeit,* two St. Louis papers he had contributed extensively to while he was out of the army. He also won election as county auditor, holding this office from January 1, 1866 until his death. As county auditor he worked for more stringent tax laws and collecting unpaid taxes of men who grew rich in the war. To the end he combined engagement in practical local politics with commitment to an international cause. Weydemeyer did not live to take part in the post-war revival of the labor movement. William H. Sylvis inaugurated the National Labor Union in Baltimore on August 20, 1866; Weydemeyer died of cholera in St. Louis on the same day, at the age of forty-eight. German-American radicals who had been won to Marxism through his efforts made his influence felt in the reviving labor movement. Among the continuators of Weydemeyer's work were his son Otto, who first translated Marx's *Capital* into English;

Eduard Schlegel, Vice-President of the National Labor Union; and Friedrich Sorge, the leader of the First International in the United States.[21] We now turn to Sorge's American experiences.

### SORGE AND THE COMMUNIST CLUB

After landing in New York in the summer of 1852, Sorge, like many bewildered immigrants, went without meals and spent chilly nights in the open air while learning to know his new environment. In the next winter he worked for three dollars a week in the New York headquarters of Wilhelm Weitling's *Arbeiterbund*.[22] After that, thanks to his good musical education and his ability as a teacher, he made a decent living from music lessons. Within a few years of his arrival, he married a young German immigrant. Comrades in politics as well as man and wife, Mathilde and Friedrich Sorge lived together for five decades; none of their offspring survived beyond childhood.[23]

During his first five years in America Sorge was politically inactive. He met Weydemeyer and gave him a report on what the German exiles in London were doing, but took no part in Weydemeyer's *Proletarierbund* or in the American Workers League. He also appears to have kept aloof from Weitling's *Arbeiterbund*, although he was inevitably within earshot of its orators while he worked at the organization's headquarters during his first American winter. In 1857, when a forty-eighter named Albert Komp initiated the New York Communist Club, Sorge became active in radical affairs. An educational society, the Communist Club was sympathetic to labor but played no role in strikes and organizational campaigns. The members stood in the tradition of bourgeois, not labor, radicalism; the immediate outlet for their political passions was the antislavery movement, and most of them joined the radical wing of the Republican party. While active in the Communist Club, Sorge also belonged to a group of radical democrats led by Karl Heinzen. Heinzen was a forty-eighter with a left-liberal's antipathy to Marx and Marxism, and Sorge's association with him, continuing until after the Civil War, was a gauge of the distance between Sorge and Marxism in the first phase of his political life in America.[24]

Another gauge of Sorge's distance from Marxism is the program he subscribed to as a founding member of the Communist Club. "The members of the Communist Club," declares the first paragraph of its statutes,

> reject all religious faiths . . . as well as any point of view not based on direct perception of the senses. They recognize the complete equality of all human beings irrespective of color or sex. They therefore strive, before all else, to do away with so-called bourgeois property, whether inherited or acquired, so that each may have a reasonable share in the national and spiritual riches of the earth, a share answering as far as possible to his needs.[25]

What this declaration shows is that the New York Communists really took their stand against supernaturalism "before all else," then against racial and sexual discrimination, and only then against bourgeois property. Their way to the good society was not through the class struggle but the spreading of rationalist enlightenment and equalitarianism. These priorities are not laborite or Marxist.

As a society dedicated to enlightenment the Communist Club was a clearing-house of socialist thought for German exiles in Europe and the United States. The club corresponded with Marx in London, Weydemeyer in Milwaukee, J. P. Becker in Geneva, and with members of utopian settlements in America, including the Icarians at Nauvoo, Illinois.[26] Primarily interested in educating its own members, the club gave little time to public activities; but in 1858 Sorge and Fritz Kamm spoke for it at a mass meeting in which the New York Communists, joined with various German, French, Italian, British, and American societies, commemorated the tenth anniversary of the June insurrection in Paris.

Coincident with the formation of the Communist Club in 1857 was a revival of the German workers' organization initiated by Weydemeyer in 1853. Rebaptized as the General Workers League, this group in its further career illuminated the tensions between bourgeois and labor radicalism in the fifties. The General Workers League adopted a platform which, in the tradition of American labor radicalism, ignored the slavery question. Its paper, the *Arbeiter*, appeared briefly in 1858 with W. Banque as editor and was notorious as the only German labor paper to advocate the extension of slavery to Mexico and Central America. There is some question as to how representative of New York German labor radicals the *Arbeiter* was. Most of these radicals were either indifferent to slavery or luke-warm opponents to it in the late fifties.[27] But Sorge thought otherwise. "The attitude of the working class toward the question of slavery," as he recalled it, "was always ambiguous." The Germans in particular, "because of the huge increase in the Irish population after 1848, either showed indifference or spoke and worked for maintaining slavery and extending its territory." In Sorge's analysis, the Irish influx and attendant competition with the Germans for jobs kept the minds of some Germans off the slavery issue, and excited in the minds of others a race hatred which led to a pro-slavery stand. Sorge did not believe partisanship and honesty to be incompatible in a labor historian, and so he wrote starkly about the mood of the German workers in the fifties, "daring not to keep quiet about it."[28] In the tug of war in which the leading German labor spokesmen and Communist Club members pulled the New York German community in opposite directions on slavery, the pro-abolition stand of the Communists won out over the traditional pro-Democratic laborism by the end of the decade, even in the General Workers League itself and the German labor press.[29]

### Sorge Becomes a Marxist

When war came many of the New York Communists joined the Union army and for the duration of the war the club did not meet. It resumed activity in 1866. In the same year a European event changed Sorge's political outlook—the Six Weeks' War between Prussia and Austria.

Before Prussia's defeat of Austria in that war, developments in Germany, such as Lassalle's successful agitation among the workers, had livened the hopes of exiled forty-eighters for a renewal of democracy in the Fatherland. These exiles formed the

League for German Freedom and Unity with headquarters in London and an official paper called the *Deutsche Eidgenosse*. In the United States Karl Heinzen kept up interest in the cause through his paper, the *Pionier*. Along with Heinzen, Adolf Douai, Abraham Jacoby, and other prominent forty-eighters, Sorge took a leading part in the American branch of the Freedom and Unity movement.

But the hope of a new forty-eight revolution was only a bubble punctured by Prussia's needle-guns at the decisive battle of Sadowa. The message of those guns was that German unity was to be Bismarckian unity and that German freedom would remain a distant prospect. Those forty-eighters who had been living on hope in exile now had to acknowledge it to be chimerical. Most gave up the idea of revolution altogether, but a few gave up only the idea of a middle-class revolution. These turned toward the workers and discerned among them the forces of a new and different kind of revolution, a revolution as relevant to free and united America as to autocratic and divided Germany. Sorge was one of those who took his disappointment with German events as a point of departure for a new revolutionary outlook.[30] Turning away from German concerns, he began to become a Marxist labor radical.

Sorge's coming to Marxism was not sudden. His disenchantment with German prospects still left him more of a free thinker than a labor radical. This turn of mind showed itself in his participation in the Order of Secularists, a secret society intent on creating a proper climate for social reform in the United States by propagating atheism. Meanwhile, the Communist Club established ties with the First International in London and began spreading the gospel of labor radicalism. For a time in 1866 Sorge was in the uncomfortable position of mediator between the Secularists and the Communists. Attached to both groups, Sorge, in the meetings of the Secularists, served as spokesman for the cause of the International, while in the Communist Club he represented the Secularists' eighteenth-century enlightenment approach to politics. In 1867 Sorge persuaded the Secularists to put themselves on a socialist footing, to join the International and send to its London headquarters for educational materials in English. When Sorge told his

Communist comrades about his missionary triumph in the atheist society, they were none too happy about it. Surprised and angered, Sorge sternly lectured the Communists that "he who is not free from all supernatural views is worthless for our cause."[31] But with this we hear the last of Sorge as a middle-class radical preoccupied with the propaganda of free thought.

### The First International and the NLU

From then on Sorge worked in the American labor movement for Marxism. As the First International's apostle in the United States, he chose the National Labor Union as his missionary field. At the outset the International and the NLU had much in common.

British and French labor organizations had launched the International Workingmen's Association at a meeting in London at St. Martin's Hall on September 28, 1864. Marx and other leading continental radicals were active in the movement from its inception. The International, as defined by its activities, was a broad affair. It promoted international collaboration among labor organizations in support of strikes and for regulation of immigration. It also favored independent workingclass parties and co-operatives. Not a world federation of trade unions, not a league of national workers' parties and co-operatives, nor yet a bureau of labor statistics and publicity, the International had functions which nowadays are usually distributed among more specialized institutions.[32]

While it was Marx who formulated the program and rules of The International, the extent of Marxist influence in the International is a disputed question. The important anti-Marxist labor historian Selig Perlman believes Marx's role was "merely incidental." In Perlman's view Marx only stated "the demands of the British trades unionists" when he wrote the International's fundamental documents. "His *Inaugural Address* was a trade unionist document, not a *Communist Manifesto*."[33] But Perlman surely underrates the role of Marx in the International and understates the radicalism of the *Address*. The rhetoric of the *Address* is calmer than that of the *Manifesto*, but its revolutionary essence is the same, for the *Address* maintains that production on a large scale, and in accord with the behests of modern science, may be carried on without the existence of a class of masters employing a class of hands; that to bear fruit, the means of labour need not be monopolised as a means of dominion over, and of extortion against, the labouring man himself; and that, like slave labour itself, like serf labour, hired labour is but a transitory and inferior form, destined to disappear before associated labour plying its toil with a willing hand, a ready mind and a joyous heart.[34]

The perspective of the *Address* is clearly not that of pure-and-simple trade unionism, but of socialism.

Marx saw the International as the catalyst of a socialist-oriented labor movement in the modern capitalistic countries. He assumed that trade-union, co-operative, and political action on the part of its affiliates would be an experience of self-education for the workers, bringing them in time to socialist class-consciousness. But Marx did not seek to make the International an exclusively socialist body at the outset; he wrote a program for it which the labor movement at its then existing level of consciousness could accept, and which at the same time was in harmony with socialist principles. This program was not a least common denominator compromise with British trade unionism. In writing the *Address* Marx put into practice the admonition of the *Manifesto* to "fight for the attainment of the immediate aims, for the enforcement of the momentary interests of the working class; but in the movement of the present . . . also to represent and take care of the future of the movement."[35]

The influence of Marx prevailed in the International's General Council and was of varying effect from country to country, within its affiliates. It was weakest in the sections of the International in the Latin countries of Europe and was strongest in the German section. In the British affiliates, the Marxist influence, founded on the rapport of Marx and Engels with labor leaders who had grown up in the Chartist movement, declined as the force of the Chartist tradition declined. Next to Germany, the most strongly Marxist sections of the International were in the United States.[36]

The Marxism of the International in America, to be sure, was pretty much limited to German Americans. When Sorge sought to carry Marxism outside the German-American community, he met difficulties in accommodating it to the indigenous radical tradition. Sorge first experienced these difficulties in the NLU. There he discovered the inhospitality to Marxism in which America resembled France, Spain, and Italy—those homelands of anarchism, syndicalism, and handicraft and peasant utopias.

The NLU, like the International, held its first congress in 1866, flourished in the late sixties, and fell into decay in the seventies. Like the International it lost its trade-union functions and grew more political as it evolved. This change in the International was not desired by Marx, but the principal leader of the NLU, William H. Sylvis, encouraged it. In 1867 a long, disastrous strike of the Iron Molders' Union, of which he was head, persuaded Sylvis that trade-union action was not the way to win justice for the workers. "Combination," he concluded, "as we have been using or applying it, makes war upon the effects, leaving the cause undisturbed, to produce, continually, like effects. . . . The cause of all these evils is the WAGES SYSTEM." The remedy Sylvis now turned to was producers' co-operatives, and political action.[37] While Sylvis was pondering the apparent failure of trade unionism, Marx was advising unionists in a manuscript prepared for the General Council of the International that

> they ought . . . not to be exclusively absorbed in these unavoidable guerilla fights incessantly springing up from the [n]ever-ceasing encroachments of capital or changes in the market. They ought to understand that, with all the miseries it imposes on them, the present system simultaneously engenders the *material conditions* and the *social forms* necessary for an economical reconstruction of society. Instead of the *conservative* motto, "*A fair day's wage for a fair day's work!*" they ought to inscribe on their banner the *revolutionary* watchword, "*Abolition of the wages* system!"[38]

Despite the similarities in Sylvis's and Marx's appraisals of trade unions, the former was not approaching a Marxist view of the labor movement. He wanted workers to turn away from participation in day-to-day struggles of unions with employers and put their energies into co-operatives and political action. But Marx was willing to accept the trade-union struggle provided unionists were not "exclusively absorbed in these unavoidable guerilla fights." At the time of his death in 1869, Sylvis had arrived at a position close to that of Ferdinand Lassalle, for Lassalle had deduced from his Iron Law of Wages the impossibility of bettering the working class through unions. What followed for Lassalle was the primacy of politics. Labor political action, he thought, should strive for state-supported workers' co-operatives as the means to socialism. Like Brownson before him, Lassalle conceived of political action in the form of an alliance between the workers and the landed interests against the bourgeoisie.[39] A new synthesis of these indigenous and foreign varieties of non-Marxist labor radicalism was achieved by Sylvis and the NLU.

The priorities of the movement rapidly shifted. At its first convention the NLU came out for an eight-hour day law to be realized through the electoral victory of an independent labor party. In 1868, two years later, the NLU launched a National Labor Reform party, but by then its principal issue was not the eight-hour day but the issuance of greenbacks by the federal government. The NLU was thus quickly to voice the traditional agrarian insistence on cheap money. Greenbacks were seen by Sylvis and his associates as the means to finance the producers' co-operatives through which workers were to escape from the wages system. Adoption of the greenback stand drew a line of faction in the NLU between unionists willing to try to redress workers' grievances within the existing capitalist framework, and those like Sylvis who were eager to begin at once the erection of a new economic framework. The Marxists soon found themselves in a void between two factions, each of which, from their standpoint, had part of the truth. They were too weak an influence to arrest the polarization of trade-union and political wings in the NLU. That polarization quickly led to the disintegration and death of the Sylvis movement.[40]

The New York Communists were undergoing an independent evolution while the NLU was taking shape. Shortly after reactivating themselves in 1866, the Communists fused with a band of newly arrived Lassalleans. The enlarged group called itself the

*Allgemeine Deutsche Arbeiterverein,* after the Lassallean organization in Germany. In true Lassallean spirit this new *Verein* rushed into politics, only to make a fiasco of trying to launch a socialist party in New York in the election of 1868. In 1869 the *Verein* joined the NLU and was chartered as Local Union No. 5. Sorge represented the local at conventions of the NLU in 1869 and 1870. As a delegate Sorge tried to get the NLU to affiliate with the International but without success. His local itself, however, joined the International in the fall of 1869. For purposes of clarity it may be well to reiterate the titles of Sorge's organization. The group had now amassed three designations: it was simultaneously the *Allgemeine Deutsche Arbeiterverein,* Labor Union No. 5, and Section One of the International.[41] Like the mysterious triune deity it had three names and a single essence; here it shall be known only as Section One.

In the first year of its existence the field of action for Section One was the Sylvis movement, but when the NLU completed its transformation into an agrarian labor party in 1870 and the national trade unions withdrew their support from it, the Marxists of Section One had no more to do with the Sylvis movement.[42] Yet the experience of being close witnesses to the evolution of the NLU had a continuing influence on Sorge and his associates. It confirmed them in a view of labor political action in America that was the starting point for Gompers' philosophy of pure-and-simple unionism. This is not to say that the German-American Marxists became typical AFL unionists a dozen years before the AFL appeared, nor that the AFL outlook was an inevitable outgrowth of the response of the Marxists to the Sylvis movement. There are similarities between Gompersism and the Marxism of the 1870's, and there are differences.

The aversion of both Marxist and non-Marxist unionists to the trend of the NLU is recorded by historians of both schools. The Commons historians, firm admirers of business unionism, conclude that Sylvis "combined in himself the business unionist and the social reformer" and was thus ill-fitted to be a leader of American labor.[43] Hermann Schlueter, voicing the attitude of the early Marxists, finds it "deeply regrettable" that Sylvis should have proved unable to avoid the pitfalls of "bourgeois reformism."[44] The difference between these two views is that one proceeds from principle and the other from expedience. To supporters of business unionism like Commons, labor parties are characteristic of young and radical labor movements that have not yet learned to adjust to the capitalist environment.[45] To Marxists like Schlueter and the men of Section One, independent labor politics was impractical in a country where wage-earners were yet in a decided minority. Their criticism of ventures like Sylvis's resemble Brownson's criticism of the Workingmen's party forty years before. The response of the Sylvis men to such criticism was to try to find a common platform with the disaffected farmers to build a popular party upon; they understood that in such a party the trade-union interest would be subordinated to the aims of agrarian radicalism; they knew that without an alliance with the farmers, labor in nineteenth-century America could be no more than a pressure group. At the end of the sixties, Sylvis and his followers were trying to do outside the Democratic party what Brownson had been trying to do at the end of the thirties inside it. The German-American Marxists opposed the tactical ideas of the indigenous labor radicals because they thought America unripe for labor politics. They thus concurred, for the time being, with unionists who thought the time for a labor party in the United States would never be ripe; who thought that labor should always play the role of an independent pressure group, a role which precluded firm political alliances, including farmer-labor alliances, as a matter of principle.[46] As the Marxists saw matters, there was no need of labor alliances with farmers and other intermediate classes. Capitalism was exterminating them and making the workers the majority of the nation.

So they waited, with more or less patience, for inexorable history to create the conditions for an effective party of labor. Socialism would become realizable, explained Sorge, "after the owners of small property will have been robbed of what little they owned, not by the Socialists . . . but by the rich capitalists.[47] In the meantime there was a need to agitate against the injustices of the existing order, and to organize workers under the banner of the International.

The first issue the American members of the International responded to was the Franco-Prussian War of 1870. They urged peace and fraternity between the workers of France and Germany. After the decisive battle of Sedan, Section One sent speakers to German workers' organizations and managed to get some unions to pass anti-war resolutions. This took courage, for the German-American community was intoxicated by the Prussian triumph. In the face of patriotic exultation, the Internationalists denounced the dynastic character of the war and warned that nascent imperial Germany would share the fate of the Empire of Napoleon III.[48]

In the course of Section One's anti-war propaganda, Sorge discovered a French section of the International in New York. By this time the war was over and the German intention to annex Alsace-Lorraine was proclaimed. The French and German Internationalists in New York thereupon organized a mass meeting to protest the annexation and to uphold the right of national self-determination. The meeting filled Cooper Union to overflowing, but the internationalism voiced was a minority sentiment. All five German-American daily papers denounced the Cooper Union meeting, and the *Arbeiter-Union*, a labor paper which had taken an anti-war stand, suffered so much from the spread of chauvinism among its readers that it suspended publication on September 17, 1870. Among the New York German weeklies, only the free-thinkers' *Neue Zeit* supported the protest of the International against the war. Under these circumstances the German-American Marxists of Section One endured isolation, not because they appeared to be un-American but because their fellow immigrants took them to be un-German.[49] This was the second time that Marxists in America had been at odds with other German Americans over what view to take of the Fatherland. In the fifties Weydemeyer had experienced isolation when he attacked the exiled leaders of the forty-eight revolution. Since then the German-American community had found new idols, the founders of the Second Reich. The Marxists. however, remained iconoclasts and continued to pay for their idol-breaking.

# Chapter 4

# The International in America

Revolution and civil war came out of the French defeat in 1870. On March 18, 1871 the Commune of Paris established itself as a dual center of power, in opposition to the provisional government of the Third Republic which operated from Versailles during the life of the Commune. The revolutionary plebeian regime held power in the French capital for two months and was led by members of the International, most of them followers of Pierre-Joseph Proudhon. The prominence in the Commune of Internationalists deeply affected the fortunes of the International outside France. Before the Commune, the International may have seemed in many countries to be a rather distant menace to the established order, but afterward it was easier to see it as a clear and present danger. The Commune, Engels wrote to Sorge, made the International "a moral force in Europe." It was "without a doubt the child of the International intellectually, although the International did not lift a finger to produce it."[1]

The Commune made the International something of a moral force in the United States, too. It evoked exceptional sympathy here. It seemed to Herman Schlueter that more middle-class radicals spoke up for the workers of Paris in the United States than in other countries. Prominent men like Wendell Phillips and Benjamin F. Butler defended the Communards, and lesser known radicals enrolled in the International while it was basking in the Commune's light.² Most who joined, it is true, had shown interest in the International before the Commune augmented its prestige. These new Internationalists were followers of Stephen Pearl Andrews.

The Andrews group, which included Victoria Claflin Woodhull, her sister Tennessee Claflin, and the veteran labor leader William West, had organized itself as the New Democracy, or Political Commonwealth, in 1869 and sought affiliation with the International. Writing in its behalf to the International's General Council, Andrews described the New Democracy as the only up-to-date radical movement in the United States and as the true heir of the American radical tradition. "Our organization," said Andrews, "can rightfully claim, both through ideas and immediate personal affiliations, to be the direct successor, if not the actual continuator, of the industrial congress and labour and land reform movement of twenty and twenty-five years ago in the country." But the General Council in 1869 was more interested in the NLU, which eluded the International, than in the Andrews New Democracy, which embraced it. The New Democracy dissolved in 1870 and reconstituted itself the following year as American Sections Nine and Twelve of the International.³ This was the prelude to a brief but fervent struggle between German-American Marxists and native American anti-Marxists for control of the International in America. This was no mere power struggle, for the two factions were at odds on significant issues even before the conflict broke out. A review of the principles and tactics in dispute affords an insight into the character of Marxist and non-Marxist radicalism, American-vintage 1870.

Sorge and his friends quarreled over more issues with the native radicals, and in louder voices, than Weydemeyer had in the fifties. Weydemeyer had opposed the homestead movement but had relented of his opposition in the crisis year of 1860. The irrepressible conflict repressed and postponed the competition of the rival trends in radicalism. After the Civil War the competition of tendencies resumed and intensified. Perhaps the intensification was a result of the postponement. In any case, the German-American Marxists now clashed with the native radicals on a series of issues which included currency reform, education, and woman suffrage. On currency reform, the Marxists met the native radicals head on. "Gold," they insisted, "is the single proper measure of value. . . . As the standard of value for all commodities and guarantee of issues of paper currency" it was indispensable to a market economy.[4] While Sorge and his friends defended the gold standard, the greenback agitation was on the rise among the native radicals, and the NLU was converting itself into a currency reform party. The Marxist stand antagonized radicals of the indigenous tradition for decades. Forty years after the launching of the International in the United States, in 1909, Tom Watson was still denouncing Marx for favoring "that damnable doctrine that gold is the natural and proper standard of value."[5]

Against the view so dear to Americans that education was the panacea for social ills, the German-American Marxists asserted that:

> The freeing of labor from the yoke of capital is entirely independent of general education. Consciousness of their position in society is all they need when conditions urge a change in that position. Necessity impels the workers to acquire this consciousness even against their own wills, for thought rises out of actual relations.[6]

In contrast to Weydemeyer's American Workers League, which advocated free public schools and colleges in 1853, this statement of Sorge's Internationalists expresses a stiffly doctrinaire version of Marxism. Marx himself could scarcely have been enthusiastic about it, for in 1876 he championed public education on the American model, "defining by a general law the financial means of the elementary schools, the qualifications of teachers, the branches of instruction, etc., as happens in the United States. . . ." Marx saw in American education a democraticizing influence. This practice was "a very different thing from appointing the state as educator of the people!" The scope for school autonomy in the American system seemed to make possible his desire that "Government and church should rather be equally excluded from any influence on the school. . . . The state has need, on the contrary, of a very stern education by the people."[7]

When it came to woman suffrage, Sorge's Section One was more liberal than other quarters of the German-American community, but it showed a lofty detachment from the struggle which could not fail to irritate the native-born feminists who formed Sections Nine and Twelve of the International. "Universal suffrage cannot free us from slavery," said the Germans; and from this premise they concluded that "the task of the workers is to draw the women into the social struggle for the liberation of the workers and therewith, mankind."[8] In effect, these words were an ultimatum to the woman suffrage movement, requiring the suffragists to put a higher value on the workers' cause than on their own. The Marxists were talking to the feminists the way Brownson had talked to the abolitionists before the Civil War. Once again the claims of disparate movements for support posed a dilemma for labor radicals. The response of German-American Marxists, like that of Brownson, was to insist that the cause of the wage workers had priority over all other causes. Unlike Brownson, who characteristically thought of party political action as the means to proletarian emancipation, the Internationalists looked for a way to improve the lives of the workers without commitment to any of the existing parties. They agitated for a legal eight-hour working day, and for the spread of unions as "the only means to avert the worsening of the lot of the workers, an end which the capitalist class—that pitiless foe of the workers—forever strives toward." But they did not view unionism as a panacea, refusing to "concede that trade unions in their present state are fundamentally bettering the lot of the working class."[9]

AMERICAN RADICALS IN THE INTERNATIONAL

It would be difficult to say what the principle concern was of the native American radicals who joined the International in 1871, but it was not the cause of labor. Stephen Pearl Andrews and his entourage were in the tradition of American universal reformers;

they were not to be pinned down. Nothing human was alien to them; nor for that matter were other-worldly things either.

By the time of his entry into the International, Andrews was nearing sixty and had lived a full life. The son of a Baptist minister in Massachusetts, Andrews graduated from Amherst College and then went to Louisiana where he taught in a girls' school, and studied law. From there he moved to Texas, then an independent republic. Andrews had become an abolitionist while in Louisiana; in Texas he took the opportunity of a slump period for cotton prices to argue for emancipation of the slaves as an economically sound measure. The Texans listened but were unpersuaded. Andrews then went to London, with the abolitionist leader Lewis Tappan, to borrow funds from the British antislavery society to free Texas slaves, but this project also failed. Yet the antislavery agitation conducted by Andrews in Texas was brave and intelligent. It alarmed the South's rulers, already tense to the point of hysteria about the security of their human property, and it probably hastened the annexation of Texas as a slave state. When Texas joined the Union in 1845, slavery there came under the protection of the Constitution.

Andrews was one of those Yankees with many irons in the fire, whom Brownson had complained of in the forties. While campaigning against slavery in Texas, Andrews, under the sway of Swedenborg and Fourier, was developing a universal science and language. Subsequently, he found time and energy to introduce the writing of shorthand in the United States, learn Chinese, take a degree in medicine, join the Modern Times community founded by Josiah Warren on Long Island, and devise a scheme of world government which he called Pantocracy. As he aged, Andrews lost perspective of his own importance and grew fond of imposing titles. The group he brought into the International in 1871 consisted of relics, like himself, of the great surge of radicalism in the forties, as well as young adventurers like the Claflin sisters, whose social radicalism originated after the Civil War.

The flavor of the Andrews dispensation can be sensed from samples of its abundant outpouring on the pages of *Woodhull and Claflin's Weekly*. Beginning in 1870, the paper carried at the head of its editorial page a list of "Fundamental Propositions":

1. The Universal Government of the Future—to be the United States of the World—the Pantocracy.
2. The Universal Religion of the Future—to be the New Catholic Church—its creed, Devotion to the truth, found where it may be and lead where it may.
3. . . . The Scientific Reconciliation of Labor and Capital . . . Universal Reconstruction on a basis of Freedom, Equity, and Universal Fraternity.
4. The Universal Science—Universology . . . with its accompanying Philosophy of Integralism.
5. The Universal Language of the Future—Alwatol. . . .
6. The Universal canon of Art. . . .
7. The Universal Formula of Universological Science—UNISM, DUISM and TRUISM.
8. The Universal Reconciliation of all differences—the harmony of the Race through the Infallibility of Reason, Science and Demonstration—The Co-operation of the Spirit-World with the Mundane Sphere—the Inauguration of the Millennium, through Science, aided by the ripening of the Religious Sentiment in Man and the confluence of the Two Worlds.

This was a richly imagined and sweeping program; and in its sweep lay its undoing, for claims to universality in a pluralistic world generally lead to strife.

In the summer of 1870, Andrews demonstrated the elusiveness of the goal of "universal reconciliation," when he responded in the *Weekly* to the Vatican Council's assertion of papal infallibility. "Rome and the Modern World of Thought," he announced in the issue of July 6, "are definitively and unrevocably in collision. In view of the crisis I pledge myself to continue to do the uttermost to found the New Catholic Church of the Future." Then in the *Weekly* of August 13, he issued a bull of infallibility of his own. It was signed "Andrusius, Bishop (Episkapos), Servant of the Servants of Truth, with the Approbation of the Integralistic Council." The following week, in the issue of August 20, Andrews declared his willingness to run for election as Pope of the Roman Church and he simultaneously proposed himself as candidate for "Planetary Grand Master of all the Free Masons scattered abroad over the world." Another week went by and Andrews was ready for a truce in the religious wars. Under certain conditions, he suggested in the *Weekly* of August 27, he would withdraw his candidacy for the Chair of Saint Peter; the conditions could be negotiated by representatives of the "New" and the "Old" Catholic Churches. Andrews was a vessel of the American genius for unity in diversity. The role he cast himself in was far from that of a ruthless Leninist splitter. He wanted to take part in "inaugurating THE GRAND RECONCILIATION; rather than the founding of a new sect." Within a year this interest impelled Andrews and his followers into the International Workingmen's Association.

Andrews' universality was as contradictory in the political sphere as in the ecclesiastical. The views of world government and international relations propounded in the *Weekly* smacked strongly of American nationalism. An essay in the issue of August 20, 1870, urged a "Congress of Nations" which would prevent war by collective security and which, in a shrinking world, would find unity easier to achieve than did the thirteen American colonies after the revolution. The logical nucleus for such a world government was the United States, for this is "the country to which all other and previous countries contribute their peoples." Because the United States was cosmopolitan, "here is formed the heart—the common centre—which shall always remain the common centre of government."

The Franco-Prussian war was interpreted, in the same issue, as a racial contest. The French were found lacking in "the principle of development which renders them fit to cope with the exigencies of the scientific era . . . The coming age of the world will be known, must be known, as the Teutonic age." On December 3, 1870, the paper carried an endorsement of the Grant Administration's proposal to annex San Domingo. "The policy of the United States at this time should be that followed by the older nations—viz., that of acquiring footholds in all parts of the world as bases of operations in seasons of hostilities." Nordic superiority and navalism would seem odd ideas for prospective members of the International to hold.

When it expressed itself on national affairs, the *Weekly* frequently expounded the "scientific reconciliation" of workers and employers to be achieved by overcoming "unequal distributions of the products of labor." Economic justice, it was hoped, could be attained without a radical assault on the class system. "Let the various producing and exchanging classes exist as they do, but let their relations be governed by such a rule of law as shall render them equal," said the paper on July 6, 1870. In a "Capital and Labor" column of September 10, 1870, a writer in the *Weekly* argued against the NLU's attempt to found a labor party, on the grounds that a ʌew party in America "should be something more than a Labor party." It should unite, not divide classes. A labor party "is a direct challenge to Capital, and it will very probably result in arraying these two interests in an antagonism which will be but a repetition of the slavery antagonism. No party built on a specific idea, looking in a single direction, can ever attain to even the promise of permanency." An article in the issue of January 6, 1872 praised "the great teachers of Socialism in Europe" for understanding that "justice among the people" requires social "forms that shall recognize the unity—the 'solidarity' of the human race." In principle, there was no place for the class struggle in the outlook of these universal harmonizers; yet when class struggle flared up in France, the paper exclaimed (May 6, 1871) that "now, the workingmen, the *proletaires*, the masses, throw down the tricolor, the flag of the empire, and hoist the flag of the people—the red flag." It was the *Weekly* which, on December 30, 1871, gave the *Communist Manifesto* its first American publication. The Andrews group tried to avoid looking in a single direction.

But it was not in gestures of support to Marxism and the Commune that the Andrews group revealed its bent. That was best defined by the campaign to make Victoria Woodhull the first woman president of the United States. Mrs. Woodhull's presidential boom was launched September 10, 1870 with a pronunciamento conceived in the spirit of American millenarianism:

> That transition from usage and prejudice which shall place Victoria C. Woodhull in the White House, is not, from now on, a tenth part as great as that from the state of opinion which existed even up to the end of the war, by which Senator Revels, a colored

man, has acceded to the seat in the United States Senate, occupied before the war by Jefferson Davis.

Immense mutations of public opinion occur now in short periods of time; and the periods of time which intervene between the conception of a reformatory idea and its realization in practice are contracting from centuries to decades to months and almost to days. Social development is proceeding under a grand mathematical law of ACCELERATION. Experience is a fool in this age. Whoever reckons upon reading the future as a literal transcript of the past will be grossly disappointed. The only way to know what *will* be is to ascertain what ought to be; Justice is now Prophecy; Equity is Foresight; Righteousness will be the politics of the Millennium; and the Millennium is about to be inaugurated.

The Woodhull campaign was modeled on the abolitionist and free-soil crusades of the thirties and forties. Mrs. Woodhull's candidacy, the paper declared on September 17, 1870, would help "convince the stubborn that we are in earnest" about full equality and liberty for women. It was this convincing of the stubborn, and not the millennium in all its glory, that was to be achieved in the presidential campaign of 1872:

We need not fear that the small results will injure the cause. The Abolition party, which grew into the grand, mighty, and magnificent Republican party, was once so small that it numbered *one* advocate. In twenty years that one advocate made it the mightiest power that has yet existed on the face of the western hemisphere. If such results grow from so small a beginning in so short a space of time, what may we not expect for the woman movement in this still later and more rapidly progressive day?

So Mrs. Woodhull and her supporters went to the political wars under the banner of Garrison and Thoreau, cheered by the illusion that they lived in a "more rapidly progressive day" than their transcendental forebears. But whatever of illusion there may have been in her campaign, there was also tactical brilliance. In her view, the cause of women was linked to that of Negroes. She argued that the political rights of women had been vindicated by the Fourteenth Amendment protection of Negro suffrage. In "Women's Right to Suffrage Fully Recognized by the Constitution," published in the *Weekly*, November 19, 1870, she argued that there was no need to work for a woman suffrage amendment to the Constitution. All that women needed do is assert their right to vote at the polling places.

Closely attuned as it was to American egalitarian and direct-action traditions, Mrs. Woodhull's argument evoked a considerable response. Leading suffragettes like Susan B. Anthony and Elizabeth Cady Stanton took it up, and it led to attempts by militant women to vote and to legal tests of the issue.[10] The assertion of constitutional rights through direct action, first proposed by Mrs. Woodhull, is now part of the tactical arsenal of such militant organizations as the Student Nonviolent Coordinating Committee, the Congress of Racial Equality, and the Southern Christian Leadership Conference in their fight to win full equality for Negro Americans. If, in the case of the woman suffrage movement, ultimate victory required passage of the Nineteenth Amendment, this did not gainsay the tactical wisdom of Mrs. Woodhull. She gave momentum to the movement and was as necessary to the Nineteenth Amendment as Wendell Phillips and Frederick Douglass had been to the Thirteenth.

The conduct and opinions of Victoria Woodhull were not helpful in other respects to the movements she was identified with. The character of this gifted and attractive woman, who was born in Homer, Ohio in 1838, was shaped by a squalid backwoods environment through which the Claflin clan moved like a small horde of locusts. They were an exploitative confederation of medicine-showmen, masseurs, prostitutes, palm-readers, and table-rappers. When Victoria Woodhull came to New York City after the Civil War, this family of sly, deceiving, and self-deceived rogues came with her.[11] During her years as a radical and member of the International, Victoria never emerged from the milieu in which she was bred—she rather took it with her, bag and baggage. The genteel suffragettes embraced her with a redemptive ardor reminiscent of Judge Thatcher's acceptance of Pap Finn. "The nature that can pass through all phases of social degradation, vice, crime, poverty, and temptation in all its forms, and yet maintain a dignity and purity of character through all," said Elizabeth

Stanton of Mrs. Woodhull, "gives unmistakable proof of its high origin, its divinity." It was perhaps unfair, as well as unreal, to expect Victoria to live up to this.

It was not, in truth, Mrs. Woodhull's dignity and purity of character, but her palpable daring and flare for the politically dramatic which won her the hearts of stalwarts of women's rights, like Mrs. Stanton. When she came to Washington on December 21, 1870—the first woman ever to speak at a congressional hearing—and asked the Senate Judiciary Committee to recommend enabling laws to protect women's right to vote as established by the Fourteenth Amendment, Susan B. Anthony declared that all the women of ill fame in New York would be welcomed into the movement if, like Mrs. Woodhull, they would speak out for the emancipation of womankind. The more high-flown Mrs. Stanton likened her to "the Mary Wollstonecrafts, the Fanny Wrights, the George Sands, the Fanny Kembles of all ages." "If Victoria Woodhull must be crucified," she told a lecture audience, "let men drive the spikes and plait the thorns."[12] The German workingmen of Section One took up this dare. They were provoked in particular by her advocacy of spiritualism and free love.

The credo of the Andrews group appearing in each issue of the *Weekly* proclaimed "the ripening of the Religious Sentiment in Man and the confluence of the Two Worlds." To bring this world and the other together would be to spiritualize politics. Just as Sorge had sought to secularize politics by bringing his society of German atheists into the International, so Mrs. Woodhull sought to spiritualize politics by drawing spiritualists into political action. "Our Constitution," she told a spiritualist congress in 1872,

is based on the spiritual idea that all men and women are born free and equal, and alike entitled to life, liberty, and the pursuit of happiness. To these broad propositions nothing need be added. . . . It is only necessary that they be completely developed in form and practice.

Thanks to spiritualism this time of completion was near. It only remained for "all Spiritualistic teachers" to organize "the masses of Spiritualists . . . to act in concert upon all political questions."

America was ready. "There is a singular proclivity in the American mind. It will always desert the less perfect for the more perfect, so soon as its proportions become manifest." In the more perfect society of the confluence of the two worlds, the traditions of rationalism and secularism would of course be superseded. "It is a false idea that religion and politics have nothing to do with each other."[13] The German atheists and freethinkers in the International did not take kindly to this gospel, but the spiritualists made Victoria Woodhull president of their national association.[14]

The "spiritual idea" of the equality of the sexes was the radical principle by means of which Mrs. Woodhull related spiritualism to free love. She thus united three common themes of American radicalism: egalitarianism, appeal to higher law, and attack on a traditional institution. Fusing these themes, she created a mystical-erotic doctrine of great intensity. In a lecture on "The Scare-crows of Sexual Freedom," delivered in 1872 at a spiritualist camp meeting at Vineland, New Jersey, Mrs. Woodhull denounced "sexual intercourse obtained by force" as the only real sexual crime. "I would rather be the labor slave of a master, with his whip cracking continually about my ears," she insisted, "than be the forced sexual slave of any man a single hour." So much for the intolerable institution of marriage. She then went on to expound the connection between spiritualism and free love:

> In a perfected sexuality shall continuous life be found. . . . Then shall they, who have in ages past, cast off their mortal coils be able to come again and resume them at will; and thus also shall a spiritualized humanity be able to throw off and take on its material clothing, and the two worlds shall be once more and forever united.
>
> Such to me, my brothers and sisters, is the sublime mission of Spiritualism, to be outwrought through the sexual emancipation of woman, and her return to self-ownership, and to individualized existence.[15]

In Victoria Woodhull the exalted and the squalid were inextricable. Genuine indignation at the social wrongs suffered by women actuated her public life, but it was also governed by knowledge of the "almost terrible eagerness of the people to learn the particulars" of sexual scandals and by willingness to gratify that eagerness in a police gazette style.[16] Eventually this charming and sinister Rebel Girl wearied of the role she was playing in America, and in the late seventies she crossed the Atlantic, crashed English society, and married an English banker.[17] Her English phase may have given Henry James a hint for his novella "The Siege of London." But if James's art imitated her life, she herself lived something like an imitation of Hawthorne's art. Like Hawthorne's Hester Prynne she "had vainly imagined that she herself might be the destined prophetess" of a new revelation "to establish the whole relation between man and women on a surer ground of mutual happiness."[18] And like Hester's Pearl she had gone to Europe to become a lady with a coat of arms.

The politics of the German and American adherents of the International afforded small ground for amity between the two tendencies and much ground for discord. Where the Germans said "materialism," the Americans said "spiritualism"; where the Germans said "gold," the Americans said "greenbacks"; when the Germans denounced chauvinism during the Franco-Prussian War, the Americans reported the war as heralding "the Teutonic Age"; when the Germans spoke of "class struggle," the Americans spoke of "the scientific reconciliation of labor and capital"; when the Germans urged "the emancipation of the working class," the Americans gave priority to "the sexual emancipation of woman"; while the Germans opposed the incorporation of Alsace-Lorraine into the Second Reich, the Americans proposed the annexation of San Domingo by the United States; finally, while the Germans, sensing a lack of consciousness among the workers of the realities of industrial development, saw no ready prospect for a socialist revolution in America, the Americans supposed that "the American mind" was prepared to welcome the millennium. Both the Germans and Americans were pro-Negro and both defended the Paris Commune, but their agreement on these two important issues provided too narrow a support for a lasting alliance between the Marxists and the followers of Andrews in the International. The many points on which they were at odds made that certain. The fragility of the International in America made it doubly certain.

In 1871 the Internationalists in America formed the North

American Federation and selected a Central Committee with Sorge as corresponding secretary. Marx and the International's General Council in London thought that their German-American comrades had overorganized themselves because the North American Federation represented "no branches of U.S. workmen . . . but only branches formed by Foreigners residing in the U.S." But Sorge stubbornly defended the new organization's right to exist. He told the European leaders of the International not to judge "our situation in America . . . to be similar to the situation of foreign workingmen in European countries." Immigrant workers, he pointed out, came to the United States to stay:

> They are in nowise regarded as foreigners or simple residents, but as citizens, the only distinction being made by calling them sometimes adopted citizens. . . . They form an important and considerable part of this country's Trades Unions and Labor Societies . . . some of the most powerful and best trades organizations in the U.S. consist almost exclusively of so-called "Foreigners," viz. the Miner's . . . the Cigarmakers' . . . the Crispins, etc. The term "foreigner" therefore does not apply to us at all.[19]

Sorge was right of course about the permanence in America of the immigrants and about their dominance in numerous unions, but he was surely carried away by his argument when he suggested that the natives viewed the immigrants more as "adopted citizens" than as "foreigners." It was a curious thing for a man who had lived through Know-Nothing riots in New York to write. As Hermann Meyer, one of Sorge's co-workers in the movement, wrote to him: "Marx was not so completely wrong when he said that we are foreigners here. If we leave aside the occasions for carousing that singing, *Turner*, and other societies offer, we Germans do not mingle with Americans in public."[20] The North American Federation was a tender, exotic plant too early exposed to the American environment. Marx indeed thought its existence there "inadmissable."[21]

Two months after the exchange between Marx and Sorge about the timeliness of the International's new American organization, the followers of Andrews joined it. In July 1871, representatives of two new "American Sections" took their seats in the Central Committee. Their spokesman was William West, a delegate of Section Twelve and a veteran of antebellum labor and land reform movements.[22] Inevitably, the American newcomers to the International pressed their ideas upon the Central Committee and the German stalwarts resisted their pressure; and while political and ethnic lines did not always coincide, for the most part they did. For a short but significant time the Andrews group constituted the American environment of the German-American Marxists.[23]

West and his faction soon discovered that Sorge and his Marxist colleagues determined to maintain the labor orientation of the International. The American feminists were just as determined not to submit to the Central Committee's Marxist majority. In the name of Section Twelve, they published a manifesto (September 23, 1871) in the *Weekly*. The manifesto defined the goal of the International as political and social freedom for both sexes, and it invited Americans agreeing with this goal to join. This antagonized the Germans, and their feelings were not mollified when West told the Central Committee that "the extension of equal rights of citizenship to women must precede any general change in the relationship between capital and labor in the whole world."[24] This was the gist of the case of the feminists against the labor radicals.

The response of the Marxists, like that of Brownson to the abolitionists thirty years earlier, was to reject the claims of another movement to precedence over the cause of labor. On the issue of whether labor's or women's emancipation was a prior need, the International split, the Central Committee dissolved, and the Marxists and feminists set up rival "Federal Councils." Both factions then demanded recognition by the London leadership of the International. Speaking for Section Twelve, West charged Sorge and his associates with having "no higher conception of the qualifications necessary to membership of the IWA other than that the applicant shall be an alien, of the masculine gender, and a slave." He also compared the regime of the Marxists in the North American Federation unfavorably with the regimes of Napoleon III and Bismarck.[25]

The General Council of the International delayed intervention in the quarrels of its American adherents long enough to make the German Americans fearful of its coming out for their rivals. Writing to Friedrich Bolte, a leader of the Germans (on November 23, 1871), Marx scotched these fears. "I was greatly astonished to see that German Section No. 1 suspects the General Council of any preference for bourgeois philanthropists, sectarians, or amateur groups. The matter is quite the contrary." Marx then went on to theorize about the difficulties the International was currently experiencing:

> The *International* was founded in order to replace the socialist or semi-socialist sects by a real organization of the working class for struggle. . . . the International could not have maintained itself if the course of history had not already smashed sectarianism. The development of socialist sectarianism and that of the real labor movement always stand in inverse ratio to each other. So long as the sects are justified (historically), the working class is not yet ripe for an independent historical movement. As soon as it has attained this maturity all sects are essentially reactionary. For all that, what history exhibits everywhere was repeated in the history of the International. What is antiquated tries to reconstitute and assert itself within the newly acquired form.[26]

Marx's letter amounted to conditional support for the Germans in the North American Federation. He was saying to them in effect: Your politics is more relevant to America than the politics of museum pieces like Andrews and West if the American workers are "ripe for an independent historical movement"; but a collapse of your effort to organize the International on a Marxist program, and to overcome the influence of "socialist sectarians" like Andrews and West, will point to the conclusion that your politics is not yet relevant to America. This was a conclusion which Marx had hinted at earlier in the year when he had opposed the decision of his German-American friends to set up the North American Federation. His judgment was most likely based on the forthright reports Sorge sent to the General Council.

"We are sorry to state," Sorge wrote to London on August 20, 1871, "that the workingmen in general, even in spite of industrial development—are quite unconscious of their own position towards capital and slow to show battle against their oppressors." He attributed the inadequate consciousness of the workers to three factors: the immigrant composition of the working class, the impact of reform parties on the workers, and the befuddlement of the American labor leadership. "The great majority of workingmen in the Northern States," Sorge reported, came from Europe thinking to seek their fortunes in the land of plenty. This was a false hope but was nevertheless strengthened by residence in this country. "This delusion transforms itself into a sort of creed, and employers . . . having gained their wealth in a former period, take great care in preserving this deception among their employees."

Workers who developed radical discontent expressed it by supporting bourgeois reform movements rather than a movement of class-struggle labor radicalism:

The so-called Reform parties spring up overnight and for every one that disappears, two new ones are formed. These parties declare that the emancipation of labor, or better the well-being of mankind, can be freely and easily arrived at through universal suffrage, brilliant educational measures, benevolent and homestead societies, universal languages, and other plans and systems which they represent glowingly in their countless meetings and which nobody carries out. The leading men of these parties . . . perceive the moral decay of the governing classes but see only the superficial aspects of the labor question, and all their humanitarian advice, accordingly, only touches the externals. Such a reform movement well advocated and intelligibly presented to the workingmen is often gladly accepted, because the laborer . . . does not perceive the hollowness of that gilded nut shining before his eyes.

Sorge presented the shift of the leaders of the NLU away from efforts to win a legal eight-hour day and other "endeavors to favor the workingmen" to useless preoccupation with currency reform—evidence that American labor leaders, even when "honest and true," tended to befuddle the consciousness of the workers.[27]

Sorge's report on the political condition of American workers described a state of affairs which afforded no scope for the International as a movement of Marxist labor radicalism. The continu-

95

ing vitality of the American tradition of democratic reformism at the beginning of the seventies, manifested "within the newly acquired form" of the International by the feminists and agrarians of Section Twelve, revealed an American working class "not yet ripe for an independent historical movement." If labor chose to engage in politics it could only do so as a dependent element within a middle-class reform movement (as was the case in the Jacksonian period). Or if it chose to conduct itself as an independent force, it could only do so by keeping aloof from the political commotion of the day and concentrating on purely trade-union matters.

Sorge and West went to the Hague Congress of the International in 1872 to state the views of the rival American factions and to appeal for endorsement. As spokesmen for minority factions usually do, West complained of the tyranny of the majority. "We have a sacred right to rebel against all despotism," he told the congress. "We do not wish other people's brains to think for us, that the General Council lay down the law for us in America." Sorge, as is usual with spokesmen for majorities, talked of the need for "discipline, submission not to persons but to principle, to the organization." He told the congress that the presence of Section Twelve in the North American Federation was preventing the International from establishing its influence among Irish-Catholic immigrants. "We need the Irish in America, but we cannot win them unless we rid ourselves of all connection with Section 12 and the free lovers. . . . Give us free play and a free field, so that we can make something decent out of the International in America!" The congress upheld Sorge against West and voted, on the initiative of Marx, to transfer the seat of the General Council from London to New York.[28]

When they got back to the United States, both West and Sorge reported to their constituents on the Hague Congress. For West the outcome appeared paradoxical. "Once more in the course of events," he reflected, "the principle of authority and the principle of liberty have come into conflict in a movement having for its object the emancipation of labor by the conquest of political power." He was sure that "the newly created despotism" would be "ignored by all American working-people."[29] In his report of the congress, Sorge rejected West's attempt to interpret the factional struggle between the two American wings of the International as a contest between liberty and authority. Sorge had seen enough Captain Ahabs in and out of the socialist movement to know that a self-reliant, rugged individualist might well "be a democrat to all above" while lording it "over all below."[30] "The sovereign ego," Sorge observed,

> when or if sufficiently strong, becomes the autocratic ego; thus naked autocracy emerges from veiled autonomy and the mystery of pompously announced personal freedom dissolves into the most vulgar tyranny. . . . The representatives of this autonomy and this individual independence are the greatest despots in their demands and in their methods of realizing them.[31]

Did Sorge have Stephen Andrews in mind when he made this generalization? That American anti-authoritarian had proclaimed his own infallibility in 1870 along with his candidacy for Pope and Planetary Grand Master of the Freemasons, and in the next year had tried to capture the International in America from Sorge's band of "aliens and slaves of the masculine gender."

The Hague Congress was really the finish of the International. Although Sorge—who became secretary of the General Council with its transfer from London to New York—worked hard to revive the movement, there was no coherent organizational activity outside the United States. A decade and a half would elapse before the European socialists would feel able to reconstitute an international movement. Meanwhile, Sorge steered the North American Federation away from "all co-operation and connection with the political parties formed by the possessing classes, whether they call themselves Republicans or Democrats, or Independents or Liberals, or Patrons of Industry, or Patrons of Husbandry (Grangers), or Reformers, or whatever name they may adopt." The Federation, he thought, should abstain from participation in elections on its own account until it was "strong enough to exercise a perceptible influence." Until then it should concentrate its energies on the enactment of laws respecting "the normal working day, the responsibility of all employers in case of accidents, the securing of wages, the abolition of children in manufactures, sanitary measures, the abolition of indirect taxes."[32] This policy was a frank acknowledgment of the weakness of the organization, and it brought Sorge and the remaining supporters of the International into conjunctural agreement with unionists of the Gompers tendency who, like them, were in reaction against the politics of middle-class radicalism. But the Gompers-like practicality of Sorge's policy did not win acceptance for the International among practical American unionists. Those practical men knew how to use a policy while dispensing with the organization which sponsored it.

Supporters of the International were prominent in demonstrations of the unemployed during the crisis of 1873, but even contact with throngs of agitated workers failed to reinvigorate the organization. Its emaciated body wracked with the intellectually empty dissensions characteristic of associations that have outlived themselves, the International eked out an existence of sorts until 1876. Toward the end, bickering over whether its *Arbeiter-Zeitung* should be controlled by the General Council or by Section One convulsed it. This dispute flared up when Sorge, feeling that the paper lacked color, got its board of directors to invite Wilhelm Liebknecht to contribute a bi-weekly letter on German affairs. The *Arbeiter-Zeitung*'s editor, Conrad Carl, took Sorge's initiative as insufferable meddling. The paper's directors did not agree, so Carl with a force of ten men from Section One occupied the paper's offices. The General Council suspended Section One, expelled Carl from the International, and brought suit against him for unlawful seizure of the International's property. It won its lawsuit, but this was a Pyrrhic victory. The paper survived only two months, its last issue appearing in March 1875; the International itself lingered and languished for another year.[33] Sorge moved the dissolution of the organization in 1875. It "almost appears to be a pretense, a leadership without a following," he told the General Council, advising them to be content for the time being to "work toward a reorganization or a new start through our circles and through our press." A tenacious majority of the General Council voted down Sorge's motion to dissolve, whereupon Sorge resigned as general secretary amid bizarre complaints against him that he wished to dissolve the International because he was an autocrat who desired a free hand in running his secretariat.[34] Sorge's later career as an independent Marxist journalist who kept out of the factional melees of the Socialist Labor party suggests there was truth in the charge he wanted a free hand, but not for the suspicion that he was ambitious to be Pope in the land of the infidels.

Sorge had his way with the International the next year. It held its final meeting in Philadelphia on July 15, 1876. There, the first International Workingmen's Association approved a recommendation of the General Council that the organization be considered non-existent until the labor movement of France could be reborn from the ashes of the Commune, and until the illegal German socialists should be free to take an active part in international affairs. With this charge to its remaining supporters, the old International expired: "Comrades, you have embraced the principle of the International with heart and love; you will find means to extend the circle of its adherents even without an organization."[35]

For better or for worse, the end of the International meant no discontinuity in the organizational life of German-American labor radicalism. Four days after the International's dissolution, a unity conference of labor radicals met in Philadelphia and formed the Working Men's Party of the United States. Sorge and Otto Weydemeyer attended the founding conference of the new party as representatives of the defunct International.[36] The new formation had about 2,500 members. It changed its name in 1877 to the Socialist Labor Party of North America. Sorge thought that it lacked promise, no matter what it called itself. He looked at it much the way Marx had looked at the North American Federation in 1871, for he inveighed against the "German imported" character of the party. The party's original decision to christen itself "Working Men's" and to avoid the socialist label was an effort to associate the group with the antebellum labor parties— to appeal to English-speaking workers. But Sorge thought this was a childish way of meeting the problem of Americanization. With young Weydemeyer, he protested the electoral experiments of the party, but to no avail. The party was in the hands of a new generation of German immigrants who tried to get the tiny SLP to apply in the United States the political tactic of the massive German Social Democracy.

Few partisans of the International who belonged to the generation of 1848 were active in the SLP in the eighties.[37] Adolph Douai was an exception. In 1877 he shared Sorge's belief that Marxism in the United States should not for the time being attempt to conduct an election campaign in the style of the German Social Democrats. "Should we adopt immediate political action," Douai warned the SLP, "our party would be in peril of being overrun by non-proletarian elements." But Douai's purism was short-lived, and by 1880 he was supporting an SLP attempt to combine with the Greenback party for the presidential campaign of that year.[38]

Other veterans of the International who continued active in public affairs occupied themselves, for the most part, with unions. Some, like Adolph Strasser and P. J. McGuire, after breaking from the SLP became leaders of the American Federation of Labor and proponents of the "pure-and-simple" union philosophy of Gompers. Sorge, on the other hand, maintained rapport with the union movement while refusing to discard his socialist convictions. His path was a painfully solitary one for a man with politics and unionism in the blood. He joined one last effort to unionize workers on a militant platform when the International Labor Union was formed in 1878; when it collapsed two years later after a series of defeated strikes, Sorge withdrew to the sidelines.[39] During his last twenty-five years, he was a student and reporter on the political and economic movements of American labor; he took no further responsibility for organized labor and socialism in America. His solitude was measured in one direction by his distance from the visionless routinism into which the union officialdom settled, and in the other by his distance from the sectarian caprices of the SLP.

Aside from the pattern of his career as a Marxist in America, the approach Sorge worked out for American socialists may be seen in his pamphlet *Socialism and the Worker* (New York,

1876). Several passages show Sorge's adaptation of Marxism to American conditions and the American audience. Above all, Sorge was concerned in persuading Americans that, contrary to common report, socialists were not incendiaries and looters but believers in the evolution of society toward a humane collectivism. "In spite of the prevalence of Egoism," Sorge wrote, "the *common* interest of mankind is irrepressibly gaining ground. More and more people unite to cultivate it, more and more associations are formed, the activity of the state and community is extending its influence over more and more objects." Collective forms grew within capitalism gradually and inevitably. They occurred in different branches of industry seriatim rather than simultaneously. They developed because of the activity of people whose intentions may not have been collectivist at all.

Look at the railroads—might they not be the property of the community at large, as well as the mail, instead of being a monopoly in the hands of private persons whose sole object is to enrich themselves at the cost of their fellow-citizens? A good many persons cherish this idea, especially the farmers . . . it must and will be realized. In this manner one branch after another will be organized according to the ideas of communism, perhaps by classes of people . . . who are inimical to it—because they do not understand it, and are narrow-minded enough to shut their ears and their eyes to everything that does not tend to their private interests.

Sorge, then, suggested that socialism in America might result from the demands and struggles of classes not animated by the socialist idea. He saw, for example, that the farmers might compel the government to take over the railroads to protect the private profits of the farmers; but this did not lead him to advocate a farmer-labor alliance on the traditional American model. "Whoever works for a living," he wrote, "has the same interests that the wages-laborer has, and should assist the latter in his struggle for the right of labor against the encroachments of capital." Any alliance of the workers with the self-employed farmers was to be on a strictly labor and socialist platform with no concession to the traditional aim of agrarian radicalism, the independence and well-being of the small farmer:

Farming in our age only pays well if done on a large scale, if large tracts of land can be cultivated with the aid of machinery and the application of all modern improvements. . . . [Socialists are] strictly opposed to the division of the soil. On the contrary, the Socialists are of the opinion that there will be a time when a number of small farmers will unite to cultivate their farms in common, will divide the products among themselves, seeing that farming on a small scale cannot compete with farming on a large scale, the same way as manufacturing on a small scale cannot compete with manufacturing on a large scale.

If Sorge was intransigent on the proper relations between socialism and agrarianism, he was conciliatory in *Socialism and the Worker* toward the feminists. While he passed over the suffrage question in silence, he discoursed on love, marriage, and divorce in terms he might have learned from Victoria Woodhull:

The union of the sexes is elevated and sanctified by love . . . But, alas! in a great many cases it is not love that ties the hymeneal knot . . . it would indicate a higher moral standard in man, if money or any other consideration were not the guide to marrying, and if it were made easier for unhappily married people to obtain a divorce. For what good can come from a union, which is sustained by force?

Sorge, however, did wish to shatter the image of the socialists as irresponsible free lovers. The image of socialism which Sorge sought to establish was that of a movement to counteract the evil infecting marriage and the family without destroying these institutions. An exploitative society, he argued, is the death of the family and the hive of delinquency. "If the parents, father and mother, have been out all day to work, to procure a scanty living; if they return home towards night weary, exhausted, there is not much occasion for home bliss." The children are likely to "get a scolding or a flogging by the angry parents. . . . What will become of children brought up in this way? If taken care of, they might have become useful members of society; as it is many of them turn criminals." Socialism would correct such conditions. "When working people enjoy the protection of their property," he predicted, "when nobody is under the ban of want, if he is willing to work—nothing but mutual inclination will unite husband and wife." Socialism "is not directed against morality and the family, but against prostitution in all its phases."

Sorge's use of the catch-phrase "protection of property" was deliberate. He took pains to establish that socialists respected personal property. In pursuit of this point he displayed a moderation which might have surprised some of the muckrakers of the Progressive era. "The Socialists," he writes, "deem an investigation into the origin of an acknowledged personal property an unnecessary trouble." Though "fraud and meanness and violence" contributed to the amassing of great fortunes, "they forbear to investigate in how much these causes, in how much others, have influenced the state of property for this or that" capitalist. Socialists "consider personal property an accomplished fact, so much so, that they consider stealing a crime." The fine print in this magnanimous declaration was that while Sorge would permit the money-kings to keep what they had, he would not allow them to add to it by any further exploitation of labor.

Sorge's conclusion in *Socialism and the Worker* was that the destiny of socialism in America was tied to that of the unions. Unionists, he predicted, "will transcend the narrow limits they made for themselves; they will expand and embrace the whole class of workers in this country as soon as they have overcome some prejudices, the natural outgrowth of their national conditions and then, perhaps, they will lead the van." For Sorge, a labor movement which outgrew the limitations of craft organization would be a socialist labor movement.

Sorge's removal to the sidelines marked the end of the first sustained attempt to make Marxism a significant influence in America. A decade would go by before there would be another major attempt. The intervening years saw a great economic and political upsurge of labor culminate in the eight-hour-day movement of 1886, and the United Labor party campaign to elect Henry George Mayor of New York in 1887. The upheavals of the eighties, however, evoked no coherent effort to transform the SLP from a party in name to one in fact. The mushroom expansion of the Knights of Labor in the middle of the decade was accompanied by the rise of the George and Bellamy movements and by a new period of agrarian agitation, but organized Marxism in America stagnated during those years. In the hiatus between the disappearance of Sorge and the coming of Daniel De Leon, the SLP was led by men who were inexperienced and who lacked theoretical understanding and knowledge of national conditions. In the eighties the SLP inevitably lost touch with the progressive English-speaking unionists Sorge had worked with in the NLU and later in the International Labor Union; its efforts to find a modus vivendi with the greenbackers and Georgites were unavailing. Its virtually Simon-pure German character was reinforced by the steady flow of refugees from Bismarck's repression of the German Social Democracy.[40]

There is no simple moral to this story. The ferocity of the American bourgeoisie in defense of power and pelf, the preponderance of immigrants over native-born in the working class, and the agrarian bent of the American radical tradition—all helped to frustrate Marxist labor radicalism in America. The ferocity of the bourgeoisie, it is true, provoked fierce rebellions in the nether ranks of society, but it also destroyed many mass organizations formed in those rebellions and disfigured the few that managed to survive. The unions that survived were not tempered in the struggle; they rather acquired a protective crust of bureaucratic caution, becoming stand-pat bulwarks of craft privilege rather than crusading agents of labor solidarity. Ethnic differences between workers and farmers meanwhile accented the insularity of the American labor movement. Industrial workers in America were more likely to be related by blood and culture to European peasants than to American farmers. This situation both helped and hindered the Marxists. It helped them play an important part in the formation of American unions, and it hindered them from making their effectiveness in unions a foundation for political action. Since radical politics in America generally signified attempts to apply agrarian nostrums of no immediate benefit to workers, trade unionists reacted with indifference or hostility to the cheap-money and price-control reforms of the farmers' movements. This reaction hardened into the "no-politics" dogma of the AFL, a dogma which came to mean no radical politics, and especially no socialist politics. It is ironic that this AFL dogma had its origin in the attitude of the American Marxists toward middle-class reform politics during the period of Sorge's leadership. What had begun as a tactical reflex of labor radicals to the trend of the NLU and Section Twelve of the International, became an inflexible article of faith for labor conservatives such as Gompers. The Marxists thus gave the AFL leaders a weapon against socialist influence in the labor movement; unwittingly they contributed to the building of a barrier against class consciousness in the American labor movement.

Looking back over the careers of Weydemeyer and Sorge, it appears that tragic inevitability is inherent in their failure to shape a mass movement in the United States. They tried for a long time and in various ways to build an effective labor radical movement. But all the tactical pathways ended in blind alleys. From the fifties to the nineties at least, the failure of radicalism rests less in the radicals than in the social context. Barring the presence of some unnoticed village Cromwell, no one on the scene was equipped to master the conditions confronting American radicalism.

☆☆☆ *Chapter 5*


# Reform and Revolution: De Leon


From the beginning of their transactions with America,
Marxist labor radicals hoped to relate immediate and ultimate
goals. They tried to select immediate objectives the pursuit of
which would speed rather than side-track the locomotive of history. The problem of the immediate and the ultimate was often
seen by them as a relation of "reform" and "revolution." In
Marxist usage a reform is an ameliorative measure which can be
realized within the existing social order; a revolutionary measure
is one the realization of which lifts society out of its defining
framework. To illustrate the distinction, the constitutional ban
against bringing slaves into the United States after 1808 was a
measure of reform because it regulated slavery, while the Thirteenth Amendment was revolutionary because it overthrew slavery. The same distinction may be made with respect to measures
bearing on the condition of the working class. Higher wages, reduced hours, and union recognition are reform measures because
they do not decisively alter the relationship between wage-labor
and capital, but workers' control of production and the abolition

106

Daniel De Leon in the editorial office of the Daily People.

Detail from a mural by Diego Rivera showing early American socialist leaders: Eugene V. Debs is in the center; below and to the left, Daniel De Leon holds a book by Karl Marx.

of the wage system are measures of revolution because they do alter that relationship.

Marxist efforts to relate the immediate to the ultimate, the reformist to the revolutionary, have sought to avoid two absolutes. The first of these is the millennial approach which affirms that socialism is always an immediate issue. The millennial approach is summed up in the formula: "The only immediate demand of socialism is socialism." An opposite approach is the gradualist one which denies that socialism will ever be an immediate issue. Like the millennialist, the gradualist sees the relation as a dilemma: reform *or* revolution. The gradualist approach is summed up in the formula: "The movement is everything, the goal nothing."

Marxism can attempt a synthesis of the vision of the millennialist and the practicality of the gradualist because it does not regard revolution and reform as mutually exclusive. It conceives revolution to be a process comprising both miniscule alterations and grandiose transformations of society, and recommends the struggle for reforms as a condition for the realization of socialism. The *Communist Manifesto* sums up Marxist tactics when it declares that "the Communists fight for the attainment of the immediate aims, for the enforcement of the momentary interests of the working class; but in the movement of the present, they also represent and take care of the future of that movement."[1]

The labor movement in which the Marxists of Sorge's generation worked was unstable and open to radical influences. They felt the rivalry of other radicalisms—feminism and agrarianism in particular—far more than they did the rivalry of a conservative, non-socialist trend in the unions. But after 1890 an anti-socialist, reformist labor movement became the most important factor in the national environment of American Marxists. Labor conservatism remains the chief problem of Marxism in the United States.

## FORMATIVE YEARS OF DE LEON

The first American Marxist who tried to cope with labor conservatism was Daniel De Leon. He sought to revolutionize the consciousness of American workers and to build a labor movement in the United States that would abolish the wage system. He wished to bring the workers along a path which he himself had traversed—from reform to revolution, and from nationalism to internationalism. From the middle 1880's De Leon's political evolution was rapid. In two ways his approach to Marxism resembled Sorge's: like Sorge, De Leon was about forty when he became a Marxist; and as with Sorge, his coming to Marxism coincided with a lessening interest in overseas revolutions.

De Leon's roots were Caribbean, Latin American, and probably Jewish. He was born December 14, 1852 in the Dutch colony of Curaçao, a semi-arid island forty miles off the coast of Venezuela. His parents were Solon (or Salomon) and Sara (Jesurun) De Leon. De Leon's father, a surgeon in the Dutch army, died when he was twelve. When he was fourteen he was sent to Europe for schooling, first to Hildesheim in Germany and afterwards to the Netherlands. In Europe De Leon received a gymnasium, and possibly a university, education. He is said to have attended the University of Leyden, but if so it was informally for there is no record of his having enrolled there. He was in Europe from 1866 to 1872. The unifications of Germany and Italy occurring in that period may have aroused in De Leon a sympathy for national revolutions. During his young manhood De Leon admired Bismarck, and the first cause to win his active support was Cuban independence.[2]

When De Leon returned to the new world in 1872, it was not to the West Indies but to New York City that he came. Quite naturally his first political associations in New York were with men sharing his native interest in Latin America. He collaborated with a group of Cuban revolutionary exiles in putting out a Spanish-language paper in the seventies. By the early eighties he had lost interest in the exiles and turned to American politics and the Democratic party. It has been alleged that in 1884 De Leon was "a paid spellbinder" of the Democrats.[3] Whether true or not it is certain that in 1886 he was enough of a party stalwart to name his second son Grover Cleveland De Leon.[4]

During his first years in the United States De Leon taught Latin, Greek, and mathematics in a school in Westchester county and read Roman law. He entered Columbia Law School in 1876 and graduated with honors in constitutional and international law in 1878. While in law school De Leon wrote two prize essays, one in constitutional history and law and the other in international law.[5]

After taking his law degree De Leon vanished into the wilderness for four or five years, probably to practice law in Texas. His enemies say he did and his friends are silent about what he was doing. The point is that American labor radicals mistrusted lawyers. They regarded them as scribes and pharisees, natural enemies of the producing classes. The Noble Order of the Knights of Labor, to which De Leon belonged for a time, barred lawyers from membership. It is understandable that De Leon's adversaries should have made much of his profession and that his friends should have minimized and obscured his pursuit of it. The Knight of Labor Charles Southeran doubly damned De Leon for practicing law and lecturing at Columbia "before law students, thus not only being a lawyer himself, but helping in the making of a class of men ineligible to membership among us."[6]

De Leon married Sara Lobo of Caracas, Venezuela in 1882. They had four children: Solon, born in 1883 and presumably named after De Leon's father; Grover Cleveland, born in 1886; and unnamed twin boys who died with their mother in childbirth, 1887 (Grover Cleveland also died that year; Solon is still alive). De Leon had been appointed to a prize lectureship in international law by Columbia in 1883. He remained on Columbia's faculty of political science for six years. The loss of his wife and three infants in 1887 may have stimulated his involvement in radical politics but did not initiate it. He had become a labor radical the previous year.

De Leon's radicalization occurred so abruptly, according to Olive M. Johnson, "that even he himself could not explain it." At the end of a New York City street-car strike in the spring of 1886, De Leon experienced a sense of identification with the strikers and simultaneously a sense of estrangement from his colleagues at Columbia:

The street-cars came in a row down the avenue. The workers had won. The group of professors hastened to the window and saw the parade go by. De Leon's colleagues . . . expressed so much contempt and scorn and even threats against the workers that De Leon felt his blood boil. . . . In this temper he wrote to Henry George that he had heard that the workers were intending to nominate George for mayor, in which case, he could count on De Leon's support.[7]

This incident must have occurred within weeks, or at most months after De Leon wrote an article which appeared in the March 1886 number of the *Political Science Quarterly*. The article is devoted to "The Conference at Berlin on the West African Question," and it shows that its author still retained his youthful admiration for Bismarck. This, together with the fact that De Leon could still name a son for Cleveland in 1886, suggests that his conversion to radicalism was precipitate. He made his hazard of new fortunes that year.

Even if it was speedy, De Leon's move to the left was methodical. He did not leap from the camp of Cleveland to the camp of Marx at one bound; he took his journey leftward a step at a time. He came to Henry George and then to Edward Bellamy before he came to Marx. When he took part in the campaign for George in 1886 De Leon was pro-labor, but he was no socialist. The United Labor party, which had nominated George for Mayor of New York, had socialists in it as well as Georgeites. The Socialists were not in the United Labor party because they accepted the doctrines of George but because they hoped the party would encourage workers to be politically independent of the two old parties. De Leon himself, by contrast, was a convinced Georgeite. Speaking with what seemed to a reporter to be "a strong French accent, but fluently," De Leon declared at an election rally on October 1 that "the large land owner is the worst element in this city," and he charged that "it is the unfortunate crushed masses who pay the taxes."[8] He remained a George supporter for about a year after George's defeat in the election. He affirmed in the spring of 1887 that the land question is "the first and foremost plank in our platform,"[9] and when George expelled the socialists from the United Labor party in the summer of 1887,

De Leon stood by the George faction.[10] As of then, Marxism and the SLP made little or no appeal to De Leon. But his experience with George and then with the Nationalism of Bellamy provided him with an American route to Marx. What De Leon found in these movements were two varieties of middle-class radicalism. Georgeism was a late form of agrarian individualism and Nationalism was an early expression of approval for the corporative tendency of the American economy. It will be useful to distinguish these two outlooks from each other and from the Marxism De Leon was soon to adopt.

The single tax on land was the cardinal proposal of Henry George. Directed against landlords in the interests of all "producing classes," this measure from the Marxist standpoint is a reform which might lead toward socialism, although it cannot by itself transform the relations of labor and capital. A variant of the single tax is the first in the *Manifesto's* list of immediate demands. Marx and Engels there call for "abolition of property in land and application of all rents of land to public purposes" as a step toward collective ownership of all productive property.[11] From the Georgeite standpoint, however, the single tax was a means of perpetuating the independent yeoman farmer and the self-employed businessman. "There is," declares George in *Progress and Poverty*, (New York, 1940) "to everything produced by human exertion a clear and indisputable title to exclusive possession and enjoyment." He was a latter-day Jefferson when he asserted that life, liberty, and the pursuit of happiness "are denied when equal rights to the land— on which and by which men alone can live—are denied." George and the Marxists had a common means but not an end.

Two months after the mayoralty campaign Engels wrote an introduction for the American edition of his *Condition of the Working Class in England* in which he made an urbane critique of the Georgeite theory. It is likely that De Leon read it soon after its publication in 1887, for it was then that he began to study Marxism. Engels challenges George's assumption that the expropriation of the mass of small landholders "is the great and universal cause of the splitting of the people into rich and poor. Now this is not quite correct historically," he gently demurs, for ancient

111

and modern slavery rested more on the appropriation of persons than on the appropriation of land.

> In the Middle Ages, it was not the expropriation of the people *from*, but on the contrary, their appropriation *to* the land which became the source of feudal oppression. . . . The cause of the present antagonism of the classes and of the social degradation of the working class is their expropriation from *all* means of production, in which the land is of course included.[12]

Engels' critique is an assault of that idealization of the pre-capitalist past which is implicit in Georgeism and other variants of agrarian radicalism.

When De Leon left George and came to Bellamy he ceased to be an individualist in economics and became a socialist. The Bellamy outlook was fully as collectivist as the Marxist. What divided Bellamy's Nationalists from Marxists was their differing views of the working class. Nationalism did not see the working class as the creative agency for establishing the good society and Marxism did. "The labor parties, as such," explains Dr. Leete in Bellamy's *Looking Backward* (Boston, 1890),

> never could have accomplished anything on a large or permanent scale. For purposes of national scope, their basis as merely class organizations was too narrow. It was not till a rearrangement of the industrial and social system on a higher ethical basis, and for more efficient production of wealth, was recognized as the interest, not of one class, but equally of all classes, of rich and poor, cultured and ignorant, old and young, weak and strong, men and women, that there was any prospect that it could be achieved.

In Bellamy's scheme the transition from capitalism to the cooperative commonwealth was to occur without class struggle; it would be the harmonious response of a united people to the realities of modern economic development. Class feeling would have to abate before the transformation of society could occur. In the transition, the working class would be an indistinct component of the general will of the nation. Conditions would be ripe once "popular sentiment toward the great corporations and those identified with them had ceased to be one of bitterness," once the people "came to realize their necessity as a link, a transition phase, in the evolution of the true industrial system." Bellamy's view of the workers and the class struggle defined the middle-class character of his socialism.

The Nationalist movement flourished briefly at the end of the eighties and the beginning of the nineties and then yielded to other expressions of middle-class radicalism. It contributed men or ideas to Populism and Progressivism and in smaller measure to the Marxist movement. De Leon was one of the followers of Bellamy, for whom Nationalism was a way-station on the road to Marxism.

## DE LEON IN THE SLP

De Leon's leftward course from 1886 onward generated tension between him and Columbia University. He came to doubt the effectiveness of the professorial role in a revolutionary age. He wrote to one of his colleagues in 1887:

> You must remember that Victor Hugo was brought up by Jesuits; that Luther was trained as a Roman Catholic monk; that Washington was a colonel in the British army; and that Bolivar was a graduate of a university in Spain. Somehow or other pupils are not always, nor even generally, disciples; besides the times are too stirring and pregnant to expect much good from the slow process of pedagogy.[13]

While De Leon was experiencing restlessness in academic tranquility, Columbia's administration was becoming restless about his presence on its faculty. Toward the end of his sixth year on the staff it became clear to De Leon that he was being passed over. E. R. A. Seligman, nine years De Leon's junior, was promoted to a professorship in 1888 after five years as a lecturer. The next year De Leon learned that he would not be promoted but was free to apply for another lectureship. The academic powers told De Leon in effect that a supporter of the United Labor party and the Haymarket defendants in 1886, who joined the Knights of Labor in 1888 and the Nationalists in 1889, should not count on making an academic career.[14] As there is no question of De Leon's effectiveness as a writer and lecturer, it seems probable that the

113

university eased De Leon out because of antipathy to his political activity. De Leon declined to reapply for the lectureship, and in 1890, which would have been his sabbatical year had he remained at Columbia, he enrolled in the Socialist Labor party.

The party De Leon joined in October 1890 was a loose and quarrelsome association of socialist propaganda groups with something under 1,500 members. The party had adherents in twenty-five states by 1896, but the membership was always concentrated in New York City. Of the hundred SLP sections and branches in 1891 eighty-eight were German. Next to the Germans the largest ethnic group in the party were the Jews, most of them recent arrivals in the United States. Native-born English speakers were negligible in the party at the beginning of the nineties. In the party's National Executive Committee, a resident rather than a truly national representative body, only two members spoke English.[15] The SLP was almost as Germanic and probably more exotic than the organizations which Weydemeyer and Sorge had led. It was adrift and awash when De Leon came into it and seemed unable to ride the successive waves of radicalism which shaped themselves in the Knights of Labor and the George, Bellamy, and Populist movements of the eighties and nineties.

For twenty-four years De Leon worked to make the Socialist Labor party the spokesman for the American working class in fact as well as name. To this effort he brought resources of scholarship and admirable native endowments of intellect and nerve. He gave himself to the cause with a passion unsurpassed by that which animated other American radicals of his generation, even including Debs.

De Leon rose quickly to leadership in the SLP. When *The People* was founded in 1891 as the English-language organ of the party, he was appointed assistant editor. The next year he became *The People*'s editor, retaining the post until his death in 1914. He was repeatedly an SLP candidate for state offices in New York.[16] He made national lecture tours for the party and took part in debates on political theory and tactics within its ranks. De Leon personally led the trade-union work of the SLP, first as leader of the socialist faction within the Knights of Labor to 1895, then as initiator of the Socialist Trade and Labor Alliance which was formed to rival the Knights and the American Federation of Labor in 1896; and then as a founder of the Industrial Workers of the World in 1905. Less than a year before his death he lent support to the garment workers who struck in 1913 to establish the Amalgamated Clothing Workers of America, the socialist-led rival of the AFL's United Garment Workers.[17] In addition to all these activities De Leon translated for the party publishing house many socialist classics by Marx, Engels, Kautsky, and Bebel; he also translated Ferdinand Lassalle's drama of the Peasants' War, *Franz von Sickingen*, and nineteen of the twenty-one volumes of Eugene Sue's proletarian historical novels, *The Mysteries of the People, or A Proletarian Family across the Ages.*

After he left academia to become a socialist publicist, De Leon's style of life hovered between austerity and misery. He accepted no fees for his lectures and translations. His editorial salary on *The People* was first twelve dollars a week and then thirty later on. Even this modest income was not regular, for at his death the party was in arrears on his salary by thirty-five hundred dollars.[18] In these meager-to-dire circumstances he remarried in 1892; his second wife was Bertha Canary, a woman from Independence, Kansas. They had five children—Florence in 1893, Genseric in 1896, Gertrude in 1898, Paul in 1900, and Donald in 1902. Paul died in infancy but the other four reached maturity.[19] Considering the means at his disposal for rearing a family it is easy to understand why De Leon never formed an image of the American working class as a people of plenty.

De Leon accepted poverty because his party was poor, not because he craved an ascetic life. It was against his personal code to make a display of his privations. Talk "about this or that man having made sacrifices for the movement must be discounted," he said.

> No honest man, if he is intelligent, and no intelligent man, if he is honest, will consider that anything he may have to give to the Socialist movement is a sacrifice. It is no sacrifice at all to invest

our all,—time, wealth, knowledge, and all else—so as to leave our
children the estate of the Socialist or Co-operative Commonwealth.
. . . When you meet anyone who talks about others making or having
made sacrifices, stop him short; when you meet one who makes such
a brag himself, put him down as a crook, and give him a wide berth.[20]

In De Leon severe self-discipline was coupled with a large capacity for recreational escape from the routine of socialist politics. He delighted to sail a small boat on Long Island Sound, to
bask on the Connecticut beach, and to tend a vegetable garden
with his Kansan wife.[21]

De Leon did not enter the SLP with a dispensation to cure
the party of its weaknesses and disorders. His solutions to the
problems of Marxism in the United States took shape in his mind
only after five years' experience in the party. In those first years,
1890–1895, he went along with the SLP's tactic of building the
existing unions and conducting independent socialist electoral
campaigns. Union work and political action had usually been
viewed as alternatives by the party in the eighties, but now De
Leon tried to treat union and election activity as polar elements of
a tactical synthesis. It was a beneficent novelty for the party to
have a leader who saw campaigning and union involvement as
complementary rather than mutually exclusive. In the course of
leading the SLP toward simultaneous concern with politics and
economics, De Leon worked out his contribution to American
Marxism.

### The SLP and Populism

The SLP began its career as an electoral party strongly inoc-
ulated against a policy of alliances with other insurgent forma-
tions. American socialist experience for a dozen years before 1890
had given it immunity to coalition politics. The experience of the
International in America had convinced Sorge that socialist political action would be abortive for a long while. Concluding that
economic organization of the American working class would precede the political, he had formed the International Labor Union
in 1878, but that militant industrial union succumbed after two

years. In 1880 socialists such as Adolph Douai had supported the Greenback presidential ticket with no tangible benefits to the socialist cause whatsoever. Then, after an interlude in which a good part of the SLP membership became disheartened about electoral failures and turned to the anarchism of Johann Most and other propagandists of the deed, the SLP coalesced with the single-taxers to form the United Labor party in 1886. When Henry George broke up the coalition in 1887, the socialists tried to keep alive what was in fact an ersatz coalition for two more years. By 1890 it seemed opportune to give electioneering under the independent banner of the SLP a try. All other ways to advance the movement had been tried in the preceding twelve years.

From the time it began to contest elections as an independent party, the SLP had to cope with the fact that radical political action in the United States had always proceeded under the auspices of some version of agrarian ideology. In the nineties the SLP effort to become a factor on the American political scene coincided with the Populist upheaval. Like the single tax, populism was a movement which went part way toward socialist objectives, but not from socialist motives. The support by Populists for government ownership of the railroads, for example, was meant to conserve a competitive economy of small, independent producers. Populists fought against private monopoly in behalf of personal enterprise. Their emergence in the nineties posed once more for the SLP the question whether an alliance between labor and agrarian radicalism could be formed which would promote the cause of socialism. Non-party socialists like Henry Lloyd and Laurence Gronlund thought it could, but the SLP leadership this time rejected the idea of a farmer-labor movement. The socialists thrashed the issue out between 1892 and 1896 when the Peoples' party fused with the Democrats to support William Jennings Bryan and free silver in the presidential campaign.

De Leon at first favored cooperation with the Populists, but he soon reversed himself and became an uncompromising opponent of Populism and farmers' movements in general. "The greatest misfortune," declared *The People* (June 7, 1891), "would be the merging of the Eastern proletariat movement into

117

that of the western farmers." The campaign manifesto adopted by the party's National Executive Committee in 1892 ridiculed the doomed farmer who was "beating about wildly, and demands mainly free coinage of silver . . . and sub-treasuries where he can pawn to Uncle Sam the products of his farm." The manifesto went on to berate the anti-labor attitude of the farmer who

> would and does mob the man who should propose eight hours' work and higher wages for farm labor; ill paid as is industrial labor, farm labor is paid still worse; and it is a bit of effrontery . . . for the Small Farmers' party to ask the working man to aid it with their votes to make the small farmer comfortable, while they themselves shall remain in want, and sweating under hard toil.

The traditional problem of the rivalry between social radicalisms was rearing its head again.

In 1893 the SLP amended its constitution to bar cooperation with the Populists and in 1894 the National Executive Committee suspended sections of the party which were inclined to flout the amendment.[22] In 1896 De Leon identified Populism as one of the "fake movements" which had "confused the judgment of our people, weakened the spring of their hope, and drained their courage. Hence the existing popular apathy in the midst of popular misery; . . . hence the backwardness of the movement here compared with that of Europe."[23]

The hostility toward the Populists developed by De Leon and the SLP sustained the integrity of the organized socialist movement but only at the cost of imbuing it with a fierce aloofness which struck many American radicals as pointless intolerance. Typical of this response is a letter written on May 21, 1896 to the SLP's national office by a correspondent with an illegible signature:

> You make a fatal error in being too *strict*—as to *what constitutes a Socialist.*
>
> Any man who believes that the present social conditions are all wrong—& that this world's goods should be about evenly distributed . . . is a socialist.
>
> Your system of propaganda—alienates instead of attracts; you

ought to receive with open arms men who believe only *in part* what
you do.

B. F. Fries wrote the party in 1895 to question the SLP's attitude
toward Populism:

> Why is it that you take a special delight in thumping the Populist
> or People's Party and forget the two big old reprobates—Democrat-
> Republican? Surely the P.P. is leading the masses on to *Socialism*,
> and that should cause you to feel kindly . . . Our P.P. club here are
> almost to a man "out-and out" Socialists in principle, and yet I am
> sorry to tell you this fact: that a year ago, at every meeting, the
> reading of *The People* was warmly applauded, now it is coldly re-
> ceived.

When the merger of the Populists with the Democrats in 1896
left him with a feeling of political homelessness, Henry Lloyd was
inclined to blame his condition on the intransigent laborism of
the SLP:

> At this moment the most distracted and helpless body of political
> radicalism in the world is, perhaps, that which in the United States
> has no place to lay its head. . . . Our Socialist Labour Party, of
> German Marxians, has never taken hold of the Americans and never
> will, for the Americans, whatever their political mistakes, are not
> so stupid as to make a class movement of an agitation to abolish
> class.[24]

Fries, Lloyd, and other critics of the SLP's hard line toward
Populism in the nineties were essentially in accord with positions
taken by Bellamy and Laurence Gronlund in the eighties; the
latter two had advocated a socialist movement which dispensed
with the class struggle and the corollary that the working class
must emancipate itself.[25] All these men were in the American
radical tradition which had seen "the producing classes" as the
nemesis of private monopoly. It was easy for heirs of that tradition to reject as alien the idea of an independent labor movement. Even after Debs, De Leon, and the Wobblies took the idea
from the German-American and translated it into the American
vernacular, its scope was circumscribed by middle-class movements which spoke in the idiom of classlessness.

Intransigence toward the Populists lost the SLP members, particularly in the midwest where entire local organizations of the party went over to the People's party. But the SLP gained more members than it lost in those years, and its vote mounted with encouraging steadiness throughout the nineties. During 1899 *The People* proudly displayed in every issue a tabulation of the SLP's vote in the elections of the past decade. If the statistics did not suggest that the SLP was on the verge of becoming a major party, they did suggest that the hard line toward Populism was no disaster for the SLP, and they projected a pattern of relations between a broad reform party and an outriding party of revolution which would be retraced in succeeding decades. Populism and the SLP grew simultaneously in the nineties; La Follette Progressivism and the Socialist party grew simultaneously in the first dozen years of the twentieth century, and so did the New Deal and the Communist party in the thirties.[26] The fact that the parties of De Leon and Debs pursued a hard line toward middle-class radicalism, and the Party of Browder pursued a soft line toward the reformism of the thirties seems not to have affected the fortunes of the three parties decisively.

Each succeeding party of Marxist labor radicalism was brought to an impasse by something having little to do with the attractiveness of the major reform movement of the middle classes. It was not Populism but the trade unions which crippled the SLP's progress. And from the nineties on, not bourgeois radicalism but labor conservatism has been the nemesis of Marxist movements.

## TRADE-UNION TACTICS OF THE SLP

The relationship between a socialist party and a trade union can conform to three patterns: a socialist party can determine the policies of a union; a socialist party and a union may adopt a policy of non-interference in each other's internal affairs; or a union may determine the policies of a socialist party. The chief issue of socialist trade-union policy has always been which of these three patterns is to be preferred. The prevailing answer has varied from country to country and time to time. Party control of unions was effective in Germany in the 1870's but failed in the United States in the 1890's. In Britain union control of the party became the accepted pattern. Some workers' organizations have complicated the tactical problem by refusing to stay in one category or another. Thus the National Labor Union of Sylvis made itself over into a party in 1870 and the American Railway Union of Debs reformed as the Social Democracy in the nineties.

De Leon's thinking about the labor movement passed through three phases; the first, 1888–1894, was the period of his membership in the Knights of Labor and his acceptance of the tactic of "boring from within" non-socialist unions to win them to socialism. The second phase, 1895–1905, was the period of his membership in the Socialist Trade and Labor Alliance and his endorsement of the policy of creating a socialist industrial union movement under the sole auspices of the SLP. In the third phase, 1905–1908, De Leon was a member of the Industrial Workers of the World, a movement of new unionism initiated by representatives of several radical labor currents, rather than by the SLP acting alone. After 1908 De Leon was involved for several years in a rivalry with the dominant, anti-SLP wing of the IWW but this did not mean a new union tactic for him.

The Knights of Labor, which De Leon joined in 1888, was the most powerful movement of unskilled workers in America prior to the CIO. Like the CIO the Knights was a formidable rival to the American Federation of Labor. The Knights were an all-purpose labor movement deeply involved in political action and producers' co-operatives as well as in strikes. They sought to organize the entire working class rather than restrict themselves to the skilled craftsmen as did the AFL, and while the AFL was plodding modestly ahead, they experienced huge gains and losses in membership in the middle eighties. When De Leon joined them the Knights were slumping rapidly. Having reached a peak membership of 700,000 in 1886, they had fallen off to half a million in 1887, a quarter of a million in 1888, and a hundred thousand in 1890.[27] The Knights ebbed away altogether before the turn of the century.

This disintegration of a great labor movement was bad luck for the SLP, for it was only in the nineties that the party made a serious attempt to win leadership of the Knights. The attempt would have been better timed if it had been made during the growth of the Knights in the eighties rather than during its decline. The SLP effort in the Knights got under way in 1893 when the United Hebrew Trades of New York were affiliated with the Knights. With the Hebrew Trades as their base and De Leon as their strategist, the SLP succeeded in winning control of the New York District Assembly of the Knights. The District Assembly subsequently sent De Leon and other SLP members to the Knights' General Assembly in 1893. There the SLP made a bloc with James R. Sovereign against Terence Powderly, the Grand Master Workman of the Knights. The Socialists agreed to help Sovereign supplant Powderly in the office of Grand Master Workman if Sovereign would reward them by appointing the veteran Marxist Lucian Saniel to the editorship of the *Journal of the Knights of Labor.* The handful of SLP delegates at the Knights' convention held the balance of power between Powderly and Sovereign. They helped put Sovereign in office but their help went unrewarded; Saniel's promised editorship never materialized.

The collapse of the Sovereign-De Leon bloc in the Knights of Labor had political meaning. Sovereign was a Populist from Iowa anxious to enlist the Knights in the cause of the People's party.[28] He could have had no interest in placing the official publication of the Knights in the hands of an SLP opponent of Populism like Saniel. De Leon refused to accept this disappointment with resignation and at once commenced a struggle within the Knights against Sovereign's leadership. The struggle came to a head at the 1895 convention of the Knights where De Leon, a delegate from the New York District, was refused his convention seat and thereupon led the socialist unions out of the Knights. The split took 13,000 members away from the Knights and left them with 17,000; they never recouped their strength.[29]

The failure to capture the Knights of Labor for socialism left the SLP free to choose among three trade union policies: It could forego further intervention in union affairs; it could try boring within the AFL; or it could organize a new, independent union movement. In practice the alternatives considered were limited to the AFL orientation and the attempt to establish a new labor federation. Nobody in the SLP in the nineties dreamed of a policy of neutrality toward the unions. The De Leon leadership opted for the organization of a new union movement. Both experience and theory pushed them toward that choice.

In the mid-nineties the Socialists came within a hair's breadth of taking power in the AFL. The 1893 convention of the AFL had endorsed the principle of "collective ownership by the people of all means of production and distribution"; during 1894 the conservative leaders of the AFL—Gompers, P. J. McGuire of the carpenters, and Adolf Strasser of the cigar makers (the latter two former Marxists)—had agitated for dropping the collective ownership demand and carried their point at the 1894 convention. The socialists in the AFL retaliated by combining with other opponents of Gompers to defeat him for re-election to the presidency of the federation. Gompers regained office and power in the AFL in 1895.[30] It was a narrow escape for Gompers and his anti-socialist politics but it was a discouraging defeat for the SLP, which contributed to De Leon's conclusion that the AFL was a lost cause.[31]

There were other considerations. In 1895 the AFL was not in a state of collapse as was the Knights of Labor, but it was not an imposing movement either. It had well under half a million members—less than half the number of workers who were in unions at the peak of the labor upsurge of the mid-eighties.[32] With the AFL so small and the mass of the workers unorganized, there were genuine opportunities for new and independent ventures in unionism. That new unions were not necessarily quixotic had been impressively demonstrated in 1893 when the American Railway Union, under the spirited direction of Debs, had suddenly become dominant, completely overshadowing all the craft unions in the railroad industry put together.[33]

Compared to their norm, the AFL presented an unappealing spectacle to the Marxists. The federation was palpably not what Marx had said a labor movement ought to be. In the *Manifesto*

123

he had defined every class struggle as a political struggle and had asserted that "organization of the proletarians into a class, and consequently into a political party, is constantly being upset again by the competition of the workers themselves. But it ever rises up again, stronger, mightier, firmer."[34] The AFL was far from conforming to this generalization. It tried to keep the labor movement apolitical, or at least immune to socialist politics. It opposed setting up a class party of labor. Its concern was not to organize the wage workers as a whole into a fraternal class movement but only the skilled craftsmen as a privileged caste. Radical industrial unionists, with some justification, were soon parodying its name: "The American Separation of Labor," they called it.[35]

Already in the nineties the AFL suffered by comparison with the Knights of Labor in the minds of those who had been in the Knights in its days of glory. "There existed in the Order a distinct revulsion against the craft union spirit," writes Henry Kuhn, national secretary of the SLP in De Leon's time:

> I remember well the zeal and devotion of these men and their earnestness, being myself a member during the 80's. . . . A healthy class instinct animated them and, to paraphrase a familiar saying, "They were on their way, though they did not know where to go." Often have I mused what might have been had the S.L.P. of 1899 existed in 1883, had it been possible to instill into that fermenting mass the spirit and knowledge of the S.L.P. of 1899 . . . enabling it to transmute class instinct into class consciousness.[36]

It was hard for such men, haunted by a sense of missed opportunities and filled with fresh memories of what the Knights of Labor had been, to view the stodgy AFL as an adequate theater for socialist workingmen. It was easy for them to decide to bypass the AFL in their quest for a socialist union movement. They began with the 13,000 socialist-led unionists who issued from the dying Knights of Labor in 1895. In 1896 the SLP endorsed the new Socialist Trade and Labor Alliance in a resolution which De Leon himself submitted to the delegates at its ninth annual convention. The importance of the De Leon resolution in the history of socialist trade-union tactics justifies a clause-by-clause analysis.[37]

"Both the A.F. of L. and the K. of L.," began the resolution, "or what is left of them, have fallen hopelessly into the hands of ignorant and dishonest leaders." De Leon seems to have believed that the AFL, like the Knights, was falling apart. The two labor federations were "buffers for capitalism, against whom every intelligent effort of the working class for emancipation has hitherto gone to pieces." Conciliation of "the leaders of these organizations has been tried long enough, and is to a great extent responsible for the power these leaders have wielded in the protection of capitalism and the selling out of the workers." This would seem to mean that the presence of the socialists in the Knights and in the AFL lent prestige and attractive power to the two federations. The interests of the workers demanded, according to the resolution, an organization grounded on "the principle that an irrepressible conflict rages between the capitalist and the working class, a conflict that can be settled only by the total overthrow of the former and the establishment of the Socialist Commonwealth." Attainment of the goal required "the combined political and economic efforts of the working class." The resolution saw the "formation of the Socialist Trade and Labor Alliance as a giant stride towards" the revolution.

> We call upon the Socialists of the land to carry the revolutionary spirit of the S.T. & L.A. into all organizations of the workers, and thus consolidate and concentrate the proletariat of America in one class-conscious army, equipped both with the shield of the economic organization and the sword of the Socialist Labor Party ballot.

This formulation was ambiguous for it enjoined SLP militants to propagate the new unionism within the existing labor organizations, without specifying whether such missionary work was to be of long or short duration. If the revolutionary spirit of the Alliance were to be carried into the old organizations for a long time, the project would not differ materially from the previous socialist policy of boring from within. If it were to be a short-term project, its application would require a series of quick raids on the existing unions followed by a war to the death between the AFL and the SLP's Alliance.

125

In practice the trend of De Leon's policy during the period of the Socialist Trade and Labor Alliance was toward open war with the non-socialist unions. This had given rise to the charge that De Leon's 1896 resolution on union policy shows the hand of a master of duplicity who managed to commit the SLP to a policy it would have rejected if it had been baldly stated.[38] The evidence suggests, however, that the ambiguities of the resolution faithfully reflected the mind of its author. As late as 1898, after two years of controversy over the STLA within and without the party, De Leon was still opposed to total withdrawal from the non-socialist labor organizations. To a socialist coal miner who had asked his stand on the matter, he replied in the "Letter Box" column of *The People:*

> There are unions in existence in which the Alliance men should stay, there are others they should pull out of and fight. What to do in each case is to be determined by circumstances.
>
> If the pure and simple organization, among which the Alliance has acquired a sufficiency of members, is run by men, who, how-ever uninformed, do not act corruptly, and which, on the whole, justifies the belief that it can be leavened upward; the Alliance men should stay there, and even try to draw into it as many more members of the trade as they can. Such an organization should not be fought; education will be enough in that case.
>
> On the other hand, if a pure and simple organization is run by corruptionists . . . then the Alliance men should pull out and fight it with all the vigor they can.[39]

There were of course De Leonists whose trade-union tactics were more rigid than De Leon's. One of these was William L. Brower, a young leader of the Knights in New York who took SLP sup-port of the STLA to mean abandoning all socialist work in the non-socialist unions. Brower sought to uphold his drastic conclusion by meeting "the objection that by organizing sepa-rately we deprive our comrades of contact with conservative workers." His answer was that winning conservative workers to socialism could be done effectively only in socialist-led unions. Socialists, he admitted, "were frequently able to arouse the rank and file of organizations reputed conservative, but . . . the old leaders, who had something to do with the bread and butter of the members . . . easily brushed away all traces of socialist agitation." Brower thought it "necessary in order to keep the recruits we were gaining, to remove them from an atmosphere hostile to us, and to place them in a Socialist atmosphere. And we found . . . that the working people were not adverse to Socialist leadership; that they would as lief accept an honest Socialist as a leader as they would a corrupt Democrat or a corrupt Republican."[40] He supposed that it was possible to insulate workers from the capitalist environment in a socialist union and to imbue them with a fugitive and cloistered virtue there. A working class which by his own admission was indifferent to the politics of its union leaders was not promising material for such an experiment.

## ATTACK ON THE STLA

Socialist opposition to the STLA grew steadily from 1895 until the party split in 1899. The opposition was organized by the able young lawyer Morris Hillquit with the aid of Socialist officers of the AFL, such as Max Hayes of the Typographers and J. Mahlon Barnes of the Cigar Makers. German members of the AFL and of socialist benefit and cultural societies provided most of the manpower of the opposition. A major union bastion of the opposition was the Brewery Workers, at the time a preponderantly German organization. The New York *Volkszeitung*, a daily paper edited by Hermann Schlueter, was the opposition's chief journal. As a minor leader of the Social Democratic Party in Germany, Schlueter had been forced to flee to America in the eighties to escape the anti-socialist repression of Bismarck.

Early in 1896 the leadership of the Brewery Workers denounced the founding of the STLA as "a disgraceful treachery against the holy cause of labor and the fundamental principles of Socialism." The treachery in this case was the act of starting a union dual to the AFL. It was an irony of history that these same Brewery Workers were destined to commit the same act of sacrilege against the AFL, although not by choice. The Brewery Workers was an industrial union organizing beer-wagon drivers, barrel makers and engineers, as well as actual brewers. It was expelled from the AFL in 1907 for refusing to give up its industrial structure. For two years it successfully fought as an independent union against the AFL craft unions who wanted to take members from them. It rejoined the AFL in 1908 on its own terms.[41] There were other instances of successful independent unions during De Leon's time as a Marxist leader. The Western Federation of Miners seceded from the AFL in 1897 and survived outside the AFL for fifteen years. In 1913 socialist seceders from the AFL United Garment Workers founded the Amalgamated Clothing Workers which flourished under the AFL anathema for twenty years before joining the Federation.[42] These instances of successful independent unionism show that there was nothing wild and unheard of about organizing unions in rivalry to the AFL. De Leon did not fail with the STLA because he neglected the sacred cow of unity.

The trouble with the STLA was that De Leon proposed to fight for it against the AFL on an issue which the union ranks were not ready to understand. Workers who were prepared to stand firm for an industrial structure—as had the Brewers—or for union democracy—as had the needle trades workers who founded the Amalgamated Clothing Workers—were reluctant to rally to the STLA on the grounds that the AFL was a "buffer of capitalism" and foe of socialism. If the workers would "as lief have an honest Socialist leader as a corrupt Democrat or a corrupt Republican," the reverse was also true. Events quickly showed that the majority of the original members of the STLA would not stay in a body too weak to protect their immediate interest. Ordered to choose between the "corruptionists" and the STLA, workers overwhelmingly chose the former. When, for instance, the brewery unions of Newark and Brooklyn which belonged both to the STLA and the national Brewery Union were told to cut their ties with the national union, they withdrew instead from the STLA. De Leon's Alliance issued better than two hundred charters to affiliates in its first three years, but less than half of these organizations remained in the Alliance until its third national convention in 1898. Soon after the convention, its largest affiliate, the

Central Labor Federation of New York, withdrew. Other affiliates either left or melted away until what was left was a small hard core of SLP men.[43] As a union on paper the STLA continued to excite the hopes of its partisans and the fury of its enemies for a few more years. The SLP stubbornly maintained its formal existence until 1905 when, with a book membership of 1,200, it dissolved into the IWW. At that time De Leon acknowledged that it had been a mistake to suppose there were enough class-conscious workers in the United States to sustain the STLA as an effective labor movement.[44]

The SLP experience in union-building was barren of practical results but it enriched the Marxist theory of unions and workers' parties in the socialist transformation of society. Meditating on the STLA experience, De Leon evolved his conclusions in a series of lectures and essays written between the time of the virtual collapse of the STLA in 1898, and 1908 when the SLP's involvement with the Industrial Workers of the World ended. It is appropriate, before analyzing De Leon's theoretical work to 1908, to summarize SLP policy on other matters than unionism in the nineties.

### NONCONTROVERSIAL POLICIES

The central concern of De Leon and his leading associates in the nineties was to convert what Henry Lloyd had called "the Socialist Labor Party of German Marxians" into a normal expression of the long-range interests of the American labor movement. Recognizing that sustained agitation in the English-speaking population was essential to the desired transformation of the party, they worked to extend the influence of *The People* and to organize lecture tours and party participation in election campaigns. As long as De Leon and his supporters limited themselves to these methods of Americanizing and strengthening the SLP, they encountered no opposition within the party and its affiliated institutions. When De Leon turned the party irreconcilably against the Knights of Labor and the Populists, the German bastions of the party accepted his policy on the whole. Everybody knew in the later nineties that these movements were dead; nobody in the SLP found fault with De Leon for writing an obituary editorial on Populism in 1898 in which he damned it as a reactionary protest movement whose aim was "to bring things back to 'American' conditions, to the times of the 'Daddies' . . . Such a movement may have impetus enough to disturb the social equilibrium for a while; permanently it can accomplish nothing." De Leon saw no role for reactionary movements in America. "The present struggle . . . is not between WHAT IS and WHAT WAS; it is between WHAT IS and WHAT WILL BE."[45]

SLP members also gave assent to De Leon's attitude toward war and imperialism in the Spanish-American War. De Leon was firmly anti-war and internationalist. Among socialists in America his stand was opposed only by leaders and journals outside the SLP. Joseph Barondess of the United Hebrew Trades (no longer affiliated to the STLA in 1898), William J. Ghent, editor of the *American Fabian*, and the *Jewish Daily Forward* took a pro-war line. *The Social Democrat*, an organ of the Debs Social Democracy, thought that "America's success will contribute to ripen the fruit of capitalism, to hasten the downfall of the economic system . . . now enslaving the world." Victor Berger's Milwaukee *Vorwaerts* suggested that the war would advance Cuba economically, thereby bringing her closer to socialism.[46]

De Leon argued against the idea that an American victory would advance the cause of socialism, in an article devoted to "Reasons for Socialists Objecting to the War." Whatever its effects in defeated nations and conquered territories, war and territorial expansion were likely to have anti-socialist consequences in the victor nation. "The new outlets secured by the war may have the effect of scattering somewhat the forces that make for revolution." Victory over Spain would open a new frontier which would have had a conservatizing impact on American society just as earlier frontiers had. "In this state of New York, the labor movement was boiling over when the gold finds of California 'reduced the fever' and thereby the revolutionary temperature. . . . Had America not been discovered when it was, Europe would to-day be a federation of Socialist republics." At this point De Leon was close to an aphorism of *Pudd'nhead Wilson's Calendar:*

"It was wonderful to find America, but it would have been more wonderful to miss it." It would have been a boon for the aborigines. De Leon was in hopes that the peoples of other undeveloped regions might be spared the experience of being developed by capitalism. It did not seem to him "necessary for a healthy development, that every inch of the globe be first brought within the vortex of capitalism. If that were necessary, suffering untold would be indefinitely prolonged." If socialism triumphed in Europe and America the countries with pre-capitalist economies "could much more readily leap forward towards Socialist civilization than by the present process."[47]

De Leon's stand against war and colonial expansion was characterized by an effort to identify anti-imperialism with true patriotism. An editorial "Word to the Proletariat of Spain" acknowledged the prevalence of war sentiment in "many of our own class, on both sides of the waters" and hoped "that this may be one of the last experiences" of a breach in international labor solidarity. De Leon insisted that true patriotism had nothing in common with support for imperialist expansion. "Patriotism, in the proper sense, means a passion to improve one's own domicile in the only way possible to-day—by elevating all others. . . . Socialism . . . alone can raise patriotism to its completest development." But capitalism was unpatriotic. "Its material needs require the sufferings of other nations, gloats over their defeats, needs their scalps, and, as a matter of course, THE HUMAN RACE BEING ONE, the capitalism of no nation can inflict sorrow on another without inflicting it on its own." De Leon knew that there were also satisfactions associated with the war and that war prosperity tended to demoralize workers. He conducted an imaginary dialogue in *The People* (May 8, 1898) with a rugged individualist who exclaims, "Just think of the amount of money that a war sets in circulation, and just think of the higher wages the workers will get when their numbers have become fewer through the accidents of war!" De Leon's response is explosive: "Horrible! . . . a social system that cannot keep itself going without periodical massacres! . . . Shame, Jonathan, upon your social system, that it

131

makes you ignorant, but makes massacre acceptable to one not otherwise a fiend."

## LESSER ISSUES

De Leon's clear anti-war stand, although concurred in by the SLP as a whole, failed to unite the party around him. The war was too small and too short to distract the party factions from their bitter struggle over the STLA. Ironically the issue which split the SLP was practically dead by the time the split occurred in 1899. Soon after its 1898 convention the STLA was virtually a husk in which SLP men doubled as unionists. Why did not the collapse of the STLA ease the factional tensions within the party? To the extent that human reason rather than human passion supplies an answer, it is that both factions sensed that the controversy over the STLA portended a growing divergence of two tendencies in American Marxism, one which was accommodating itself to the Gompers hierarchy of the AFL and the other which was settling into implacable opposition to that hierarchy. Meanwhile, with the disappearance from view of the immediate principal issue dividing them, the De Leonists and anti-De Leonists found other things to fight about. They quarreled over Americanizing the party, over proletarian and middle-class influences in the party, over control of the socialist press, and over the behavior of De Leon as a party leader.

To De Leon Americanization meant an effort to make the SLP independent of the German Social Democracy in matters of program and tactics. Because of the heavy proportion of Germans in its membership, the SLP lived in the shadow of the mighty German party more than did other parties of the Second International. If De Leon's adversaries attacked his policies for deviating from the German norm, he upbraided his critics for "attempting to make the Party in this country subordinate to the Party in Germany."[48] In pitting himself against the *alte deutschen Genossen* of the SLP De Leon felt that he was opposing men who, having "evoked no response" from the American people, "shrank into social clubs—singing and drinking and card-playing societies,

132

with an occasional outing when a member dies, and periodical cele-
brations in which thrilling speeches were delivered by themselves
to themselves." They seemed to him to be more interested in socialism abroad than at home. "A movement such as ours," he insisted, "can be truly at the heart of those to whom, whether born
here or not, America is their home. . . . To all others the movement can only be a sport or pastime." His faction was different,
was not "in the movement for the fun of the thing." For De Leon
the distinction between politics as a vocation and as a game was
firm, and for him the idea of high seriousness in politics and
Americanizing the socialist movement were inseparable.

The idea of politics as a vocation is tied to the issue of
middle-class influence in the SLP's factional convulsion. To those
acquainted with the patterns of factional warfare within Marxian
organizations it will be no surprise that De Leon considered his
opponents unproletarian as well as insufficiently American in
their interests. He thought the outlook of the opposition expressed
"the changing angle of vision of the former workingman who had
become bourgeois" where it did not express the ideology of business unionism in which "all sense of solidarity vanished."[49]
Whether or not De Leon's class analysis of the opposition was
accurate, a conservative, business-oriented officialdom was en-
trenching itself in the American trade unions during the period
when De Leon thought he detected a similar trend in the SLP.[50]

As both De Leon and the opposition strove to win a majority
of the party to their respective views, a dispute arose between the
two factions about the proper relation between the party and its
press. The dispute involved three papers—two weeklies, *The
People* and the *Vorwaerts*, and one daily, the *Volkszeitung*. The
*Vorwaerts*, like *The People*, was controlled by De Leon; the
*Volkszeitung* was controlled by the opposition. The *Vorwaerts*
was directed to a national readership and the *Volkszeitung* to a
local New York one. In order to get its views out to the party
nationally the opposition pre-empted the mailing list of *The
People* and inserted a supplement of its own into the *Vorwaerts*.
The De Leonist party leadership asserted their exclusive right to
dispose of the mailing list of *The People* and the content of the

*Vorwaerts.* The opposition contended that such matters ought really to be in the hands of the opposition-controlled Socialistic Co-operative Publishing Association, from whose presses the party papers were printed.

"You see," the directors of the publishing house explained, "our Association has always been and now is the sole owner of both *The People* and the *Vorwaerts* and everything connected with them, including the mailing list as well as the right of issuing said organs in any form it may desire, and with or without supplement, as it may think best." The SLP National Executive Committee responded that "the Party as a whole" was "a safer guardian of its own principles" because other organizations "are liable to change for the worse, whereas the S.L.P. is by its very nature an unchangeable and true body, ever young, ever self-purifying, ever growing in knowledge and strength." The Socialistic Co-operative Publishing Association, by contrast, was "a body which the Socialist spirit has fled and the 'bourgeois' spirit of property invaded." Against the Association's claim to sole ownership and control of the party press the De Leonist expostulated: "When was a greater insolence the accompaniment of bolder assumptions?"[51] But by its assertion of the incorruptibility of the party, the leadership demonstrated that the opposition had no monopoly on arrogance. What both sides were saying revealed a split past mending.

The struggle over control of the party press had an abiding influence. When the anti-De Leon wing of the SLP merged with the Debsians in 1901 to form the Socialist party it carried into the new organization its favorable attitude toward the autonomy of the socialist press, and so helped define the characteristic relationship between the Socialist party and its allied periodicals. SP journalism was as variegated in opinion and policy as was the membership of the SP itself. The SLP, in contrast, developed a party-line press which was bound to defend the governing policies of the party.[52]

De Leon's conduct as a leader was an opposition issue, just as the alleged middle-class or business-unionist mentality of the opposition was a De Leonist issue. Morris Hillquit was "repelled by" De Leon's "dictatorial demeanor, so utterly misplaced in a voluntary and democratic movement." The *Volkszeitung* at the height of the factional crisis represented De Leon as an overbearing dance-master, calling out and piping the steps and turns for his corps de ballet:

Ordonanzen, Ordonanzen!
Die Sektionen muessen tanzen
    Wie ich ihnen aufgespielt.
Eins-Zwei-Drei und Runde, Runde!
Lernet Disziplin begreifen
Euer Fuehrer wird Euch pfeifen
    Und Ihr werdet ihn verstehn.
Immer streifer, immer strammer,
Hoch die Hand und hoch die Hammer!
    Rings um mich sollt Ihr Euch drehn.[53]

The De Leonists parried such thrusts at their leader. "Bitter personalities are indulged in," they argued, "because the great fact is not yet generally comprehended—or is too frequently lost sight of by those even who comprehend it—that social movements, or diverging tendencies within those movements, are not the product of their so-called leaders, but the inverse proposition is true. The existence of differences is therefore, as a rule, wrongly imputed to" the leaders of factions.[54] The De Leonists were probably right to view the party crisis as the result of a widening rift between diverging tendencies rather than as a product of the imperiousness and truculence of their leader. But De Leon was more than a representative of his faction. He shaped as well as expressed a tendency.

From the split in the SLP both factions lost assets neither side ever recovered. The split thrust De Leon into prophetic isolation from what quickly became the main organization of American labor radicalism in the years before the Russian Revolution. The new Socialist party, in turn, was largely deprived of the influence of the most original and gifted Marxist thinker in America. However unavoidable and desirable it may have appeared to both sides, the split in the SLP served the cause of Marxism in the United States badly. It tended to group American socialists according to whether they valued practicality or theoretical acumen more, and according to whether they tended to see the American working class as it was or to see it as it ought to have been. The practical achievements of the Debsian SP having been exhaustively studied elsewhere, De Leon's theoretical achievements in developing an American adaptation of Marxism are now considered.

### THEORY OF PARTY ORGANIZATION

De Leon emerged from the struggle with the opposition convinced that an effective socialist party must be composed of straight-laced revolutionaries only. This conviction was associated in his mind with an image of the United States as the one major country in the world preeminently ripe for socialism. "No other country is ripe for the execution of Marxian revolutionary tactics," he insisted. The fact that socialist movements in Europe were far larger than his own did not dissuade him, and when August Bebel assumed that Germany would most likely take "the leading role in the pending revolution," De Leon disagreed. "Germany," he maintained, "is almost half a revolutionary cycle behind" the United States. "Her own bourgeois revolution is but half achieved," and Germany would not be able to jump from feudal-bureaucratic capitalism into socialism without passing through the stage of democratic capitalism. Only through the intervention of already established socialist nations could Germany hope to skip a historical stage; she could not "perform the same feat alone, unaided."

No, thought De Leon, for Germany the only practical aim at present was "the completion of the capitalistic revolution, first of all." Geography as well as social structure suggested this answer:

Whatever doubt there can be as to Germany's ripeness, there can be none as to the utter unripeness of all other European countries with the single exceptions of France and Belgium,—and surely none as to Russia . . . The masses would be mobilized from the surrounding hives of the Cimmerian darkness of feudo-capitalism, and they would be marched convergently with as much precision and dispatch upon the venturesome leader. And what is true of Germany on this head is true of any other European country.[55]

De Leon's idea of the hopelessness of isolated, single-country revolutions on the European continent went back to Marx who had called in 1848 for a revolutionary war against Czarist Russia to save the democratic revolutions in Germany, Hungary and France;[56] in the *Manifesto* Marx had declared that "united action of the leading civilized countries at least, is one of the first conditions for the emancipation of the proletariat." De Leon made Marx's ideas about the preconditions of socialism in Europe serve his view that the United States was more favorably situated for the conduct of radical social experimentation than any European country.

De Leon's thinking about America's role in the world revolution, and his related attitude toward European Social Democratic parties, was complex and changeable. In his thinking about America he made a series of efforts to arrive at an understanding of the country which would reconcile his belief in the imminence of revolution here with the fact that American workers were unprepared for revolutionary action. In his thinking about Europe he made a series of efforts to comprehend the meaning of an imposing socialist movement on a continent which afforded that movement no prospects of early success. His view of European Social Democracy evolved from respect to disgust to tolerant condescension.

### De Leon and European Socialism

European, in particular German, Marxism was highly regarded by De Leon in the earlier years of his Marxist career. In the nineties he translated and "adapted to America," as the title pages declare, five of Karl Kautsky's programmatic essays. In 1892 he brought out Engels' *Socialism: Scientific and Utopian*, and in 1898 Marx's *Eighteenth Brumaire of Louis Bonaparte*. As late as 1898 *The People* hailed "the German movement" as an "inspiring portent" of the work the SLP was now doing.

With the turn of the century came a sharp change in De Leon's attitude toward the European movement. Three events changed his mind—the rise of Eduard Bernstein's Revisionism in the German party, the crisis among the French socialists occasioned by the entry of Alexandre Millerand into a bourgeois government, and Kautsky's conciliation of the supporters of Millerand's tactics.

Revisionism owed its name to the circumstance that it originated in a review and rejection of the Marxist theory of growing alienation of labor under capitalism, and of the concomitant theory that intensified class struggle would lead to social crisis and ultimately to socialist revolution. Revisionism counterposed to the revolutionary perspective an evolutionary pattern of the gradual growing over of capitalism into socialism through an accretion of ameliorative reforms. The process would be characterized by collaboration between classes rather than by struggle.

When Revisionism came to De Leon's attention he was immediately hostile. "Bernstein's views," he suggested in 1898, were attributable to his years of exile in England; he must have "lost his bearings when he landed in the atmosphere of English speaking politics, where, differently from on the continent, everything contributes to confuse and blur the lines of the revolutionary movement." Like Brownson De Leon was certain that Europe was a good nursery of revolutionary theory even if it was not a good theater of revolutionary action. The Anglo-Saxon world was another matter. There the ruling class employed "greater chicanery" in dealing with the representatives of the workers while on the continent "not even for the sake of obtaining political safety does it condescend to associate with" the workers. "Theodore Roosevelt invited union leaders to lunch, the Kaiser did not. Capitalism, together with all the chicanery that the word implies, permeates the English speaking world; hence the problem before the Socialist is there the most difficult. . . . Hence we may, we must be prepared to see the movement in the English speaking world, for a time, lag far behind that on the continent."[57] At this point De-Leon's faith in the revolutionary integrity of the European movement was based on the consideration that the tautness of European class lines would prevent its going soft.

Socialist controversy over Millerand's entry into a French government paralleled the theoretical wrangle over evolution and revolution occasioned by Revisionism. Millerand entered a cabinet of bourgeois republicans because of a seeming threat to the Third Republic from the clerical and royalist right wing. Millerand's motive was to save democracy but the performance of the government he joined caused many socialists to look upon Millerand's membership as an act of treason to socialism. Ostensibly called into power to protect France from a rightist coup, the government turned its guns on the left, sending troops to put down strikes in Chalon and on the island of Martinique. Millerand accepted moral responsibility for these actions by remaining in the government. His conduct was debated throughout the socialist movement and became the principal issue before the International Socialist Congress in Paris in 1900[58]

At the congress the French Marxists led by Jules Guesde condemned Millerand and "ministerialism." The French reformists led by Jean Jaures asked the congress to uphold Millerand. The issue was disposed of through the good offices of Kautsky and the German delegation. Kautsky wrote a resolution for the congress which shelved rather than settled the issue. "Accession of an isolated Socialist to a capitalist government" Kautsky characterized as "an expedient, imposed, transitory, exceptional." His resolution called such a step "a question of tactics and not of principle," and it concluded that "a Socialist must leave the ministry when the organized party recognizes that the government gives evidence of partiality in the struggle between capital and labor."[59] This was very diplomatic. The congress did not pass judgment on whether Millerand should have joined the cabinet in the first place and favored his withdrawal if, in the opinion of the "organized party," the government was strike-breaking. Since there was more than one "organized party" of socialism in France and since these parties were divided over whether Millerand should have become a cabinet minister, there was no way of applying the resolution of the congress to the case in question.

To De Leon, Kautsky's diplomatizing at the Paris congress was a sign that the revolutionary protestations of the German Social Democracy should not be taken too seriously. It now dawned on him that the tendency represented by Bernstein was not so alien to continental socialism as he had supposed in 1898. Marxism was not really better situated in Europe than in America, he concluded. "Once imagined to spread at least over the continent of Europe, with weak imitations in America, militant Socialism now discovers that it is a force in spots only, with France in the lead, and that America is one of its strongholds." De Leon now took a despairing view of the other parties. "East and West, in Europe as in America, the Social Democracy is a ship no Socialist can take passage on. It is bound to suffer shipwreck."[60] Meanwhile Victor Berger, a helmsman of the newly organized Socialist party, affirmed that "the tactic of the American Socialist Party, if that party is to live and succeed—can only be the much abused and much misunderstood Bernstein doctrine."[61]

In the four years between the Paris and Amsterdam Congresses of the Second International De Leon composed his feeling about the outbreak of Revisionism in the European Socialist movement. When he went to Amsterdam in 1904 as the SLP's delegate to the congress he was no longer indignant about the course of the European parties. It was no tragedy that they were proving incapable of pursuing a revolutionary course since Europe was not ready for a socialist revolution anyway. De Leon's new tolerance for gradualism in a European context is shown in his analysis of the 1903 congress of the German party at Dresden.

To De Leon the Dresden Congress revealed that the German party had "ceased to be a pace-setter for the Socialist movement of the world." History had forced it to "face and solve the issues left unfaced and unsolved by the nation's bourgeoisie." What was going on in the German Social Democracy was illustrated by the paradoxical behavior of the Marxist and revisionist factions at Dresden. The delegates had spent five days debating acrimoniously over tactics. An overwhelming majority endorsed the Marxists and rejected the Revisionists. The paradox was that the victors did not behave like victors nor the vanquished like vanquished.

The majority, emotionally committed to Marxism, was inclined to rant. "The serenest of the disputants, the most goodnatured, those who, with the greatest moderation, and dignity withal, retorted to the vehement onslaughts against them, were that nominally trivial minority." The advocates of reformist tactics were serene because "all the facts, hence all the arguments applicable to the situation, were on that side. They knew themselves the victors."

The principal debaters at Dresden were Georg von Vollmar, August Bebel, and Karl Kautsky; in them De Leon saw personified the right, the left, and the center of the German party. De Leon characterized Vollmar as an "intelligent or sentient" leader who "has adapted his conduct to local exigencies." What Vollmar adapted to was the fact that "in Germany, bona fide reform could and can be wrung from the possessing classes for the working class." Where this was the case one did not have to be revolutionary to do effective work for the cause of progress.

> On the contrary, where such reforms are possible, they are so just because a true Socialist movement is not yet possible—a feudal class, still mighty, though crowded by its upstart rival, the capitalist, . . . will lend a helping hand to what instinctively it feels to be its rising rival's predestined slayer. SO LONG AS SUCH REFORMS ARE TO BE GAINED, THEY SHOULD BE STRIVEN FOR; but so long as they are to be gained, the struggle is not yet between Socialism and private property in natural and social opportunities.

Here De Leon was restating the tactic of using the junker and planter enemies of the workers' enemies, the tactic of Lassalle in Germany and Brownson in America. De Leon was willing to let Vollmar and the Social Democratic right wing make use of the tactic to deal with the occasions and opportunities of their time and country. Vollmar, he said, "is not a revolutionary Socialist. What else Vollmar might be elsewhere, he can be none in Germany."

Toward Bebel as the representative of the Marxist left in Germany De Leon showed a compassion verging on the elegiac:

> Infinitely more sympathetic than the practical Vollmar, Bebel . . . has failed to subordinate his ideal to the circumstances. His fires

141

proved proof against facts. Though banked they have never been extinguished. Always heating the mass, that in the end, ever prevailed against them, and thus ever imparting a glamor to his party, they periodically would break and leap forth in tongues of lambent flame—soul-stirring warning. But their language could be none other than that of protest. Periodically, when a new shoot downward was shot in its course by the current that Bebel was constrained to drift with, a new shock was felt. Ever at such recurring periods, the reminiscence and ideals of his own and his party's youth would reassert themselves. . . . And then—as happened regularly before, and poetically expressed by Vollmar—the ingredients of the alleged poisoned chalice would be quaffed anew and found palatable, and the "poison" label would be transferred to some fresh cup: the Bebel-swollen flood of the nominal majority would again recede; the Vollmar ebb of the nominal minority would return and resume control.

The riot of metaphor brought together by De Leon in this depiction of an aging revolutionary faithful to his dream but helplessly swept over the rapids while tasting reformist poison, attests how deeply affecting Bebel's predicament was to De Leon. It was a predicament which De Leon strove to avoid for himself and which he imagined he had been spared. In fact the destinies of Bebel and De Leon were not dissimilar. It was De Leon's fate to stand outside the mainstream of American labor and to be unable to change its course. And it was the fate of Bebel to live within the mainstream of German labor and to fail, in the end, to give it a revolutionary direction.

Between Bebel and Vollmar in the German party De Leon saw a center group "devoid of the practical sense of a Vollmar that tends to solidify ideals, devoid of the moral and mental exaltation of a Bebel that tends to idealize the practical." To the center belong the "theorickers, who riot in theory. . . . The type of this group is Kautsky: its feature is 'to run with the hares and bark with the hounds'." De Leon saw more significance in Kautsky's conciliation of the Millerandists at the Paris Congress than in the Marxist rhetoric with which he supported Bebel at Dresden. "At the Paris Congress an anti-Millerandist attitude was decidedly unpopular; there Kautsky was 'running with the hares.'" At Dresden Kautsky was "again to the fore, but now barking with the hounds." De Leon discovered that he shared his response to Kautsky's conciliatory resolution on Millerandism with the Russian Marxists. He noted that "*Iskra*, the organ of the Russian Social Democratic Labor party, wittily satirized both author and resolution as the 'Kaoutchouc (India rubber) resolution.' "[62]

## DE LEON AND AMERICAN REFORMISM

How could De Leon be tolerant of reformism in the German socialist movement while remaining dead set against the parallel drift of the American movement? In general he thought that a country like the United States, where feudal institutions had never existed or had been eliminated, was ready for a more sweeping variety of social change than could be contemplated for benighted Germany. Ready in what sense? In the answer is the essence of De Leon's adaptation of Marxism to America.

At the Amsterdam Congress De Leon described the American political scene as it looked to him in 1904. "The moment feudalism is swept aside, and capitalism wields the scepter untrammeled, as here in America—from that moment the ground is ready for revolution to step on; what is more, from that moment reform becomes a snare and a delusion."[63] The ground was ready but not the men: De Leon had no hallucinations about the frame of mind of the American workers.

De Leon's report to the congress appraised social relations in the United States as they had developed in the half century since Marx in the *Eighteenth Brumaire* had characterized the American republic as a conservative form of bourgeois society. Had the prodigious growth of half a century ended, leaving America with a stable class system like Europe's? Not according to De Leon. Even if the frontier had vanished the westward movement was still in progress. The center of population, in western Virginia in 1850, was now in Indiana; the center of manufacturing, in Pennsylvania in 1850, was now in central Ohio. The movement would continue. Furthermore, machinery and methods of production, discarded in more advanced centers, are constantly reappearing in less advanced localities, carried thither by the flux of our population westward. . . . not only is the population still not "stagnant," . . . but . . . still the odd phenomenon is visible in America of families with members in all classes, from the upper plutocratic class, down through the various gradations of the middle class, down down to the "house-and-lot"-owning wage slave in the shop, and even further down to the wholly propertyless proletariat.

As for the immigrants,

if one-half of the Europeans, now located in Greater New York, and who in their old homes pronounced themselves Socialists, remained so here, the Socialist organization in the city alone would have not less than 25,000 members. Yet there is no such membership or anything like it. The natives' old illusions regarding material prospects draw the bulk of the immigrants into their vortex.

The United States, then, was a nation of continuing economic dynamism and intellectual complacency, "still traveling in the orbit that Marx observed it in, during 1852." American conditions, thought De Leon, precluded a large Marxist movement such as "capitalist development might at first blush lead the casual observer into expecting." American conditions instead continued to provide field days for a series of radical reform movements like the Single Tax, Populism, and the municipal reformism of Victor Berger. They would have, were having, their long day. But "capitalist development in America is now steadily overtaking and overcoming the obstacles that Marx enumerated for the conservative form of the American bourgeois republic to enter upon its political revolutionary form. . . . The backwardness of the Socialist movement in America is on the surface only." Meanwhile De Leon wished that the Socialist Labor party be judged by the quality of its ideas rather than by the breadth of its influence. He did not expect that the value of his party's educational work would be understood by "the successive waves of alleged revolutionary movements and American reformers generally, who with the tenacity of a disease turn up and turn down the country's political stage."[64]

144

Reformism was infesting the American body politic like a stubbornly lingering disease and—to follow De Leon's mixed figure —the revolutionaries were waiting impatiently in the wings. De Leon thought the moment for the entrance of the new actors would be soon. The cues of imminent change in the American situation had been given. It seemed that the American workers were about to move. The coal miners' strike of 1902 was a good omen. "When three years ago the miners' strike took place," De Leon told the delegates to the founding of the IWW in 1905, "it was, as far as I was concerned individually, an epoch in my existence. Before that I was certain that the emancipation of the working class . . . was a possibility." The strike revealed a working class sufficiently organized to shake the economy of the nation. Had a powerful, radical industrial union movement then existed, "the revolution would have been accomplished in 1903. The workingmen's pulse beat high. The class instinct was there; the revolutionary spirit was there; but the army of labor, like the Czar's army, which also consisted of workingmen, was captained by the lieutenants of the capitalist class."[65]

The significance of this statement hinges on what is meant by "revolution." If De Leon meant a radical shift in labor consciousness and the rapid growth of a new workers' movement, he was at least conjuring with possibilities; but if he wished to convey that only the hierarchy of the AFL stood between American capitalism and its overthrow in the year 1903, he had left terra firma to soar in the realm of convention hyperbole. In any case, revolutionaries like De Leon were not alone in sensing that the miners' strike had a historic meaning. "The anthracite coal strike of 1902 was doubtless the most important event in the history of American trade unionism until that time," writes Selig Perlman.

For the first time a labor organization tied up for months a strategic industry . . . without being condemned as a revolutionary menace to the existing social order calling for suppression by the government. . . . The public identified the anthracite employers with the trust movement, which was then new and seemingly bent on uprooting the traditional free American social order; by contrast the striking miners appeared almost as champions of Old America.[66]

For De Leon this kind of national impact together with the sharp disappointment among the miners at the arbitration award of Theodore Roosevelt's Coal Strike Commission meant that an opportunity was present to replace the conservative unions with new revolutionary unions. In the United States it was time to supplant men like Gompers and John Mitchell of the United Mine Workers, while in Germany it was still opportune to tolerate the authority of moderate laborites like Vollmar.

Paradoxically the man who believed this assumed at the same time that American workers were less politically conscious than their European counterparts. "The tablets of the minds of the European, especially the Continental working classes," declared De Leon in 1896,

> have lines traced upon them by the master hands of the ages. . . . But here, one charlatan after another . . . would go among the people and upon the minds of the working classes scribble his crude text. . . . The charlatans, one after the other, set up movements that proceeded upon lines of ignorance; . . . All these movements came to grief, and what was the result?—disappointment, stagnation, diffidence, hopelessness in the masses.[67]

At the same time he believed that the workers through revolutionary "instinct" and "spirit" would transcend traditional confusion to arrive at a consciousness which would change the world.

De Leon in the nineties had sought to use a revolutionary union, the STLA, to drive a wedge between the American workers and the AFL leadership. As matters turned out, however, the AFL leadership, through the STLA, drove a wedge between the majority of American socialists and De Leon. That was the meaning of the SLP split of 1899. It took a little while for De Leon to understand it this way. There can be no doubt that at first he believed the split would be for the good of the movement. It seemed to him a decisive step in changing the SLP from a weak propaganda circle of aliens to an effective American party. "Ten years ago," he wrote in *The People* (July 23, 1899), "the Socialist Labor Party was a 'Party' in name only. It is essential to a political party, first, that it be a pulsation of the national life . . . and secondly, that it be politically active. That which ten years ago called itself the 'Socialist Labor Party,' lacked both essentials." But a decade of electoral and union activity had wrought a qualitative change and the SLP had "become a party indeed."

Emerging from the split filled with optimism, De Leon entered the new century with high hopes. A brilliant future awaited the party, he told the delegates to the 1900 convention:

> Economic and political development have gone on in a way that clears the field in America as it clears it in no other country under the sun. Not only are the two capitalist parties, the one of uncompromising capitalism, the other of alleged revolution—the Democratic Party—not only are they here clear cut, but they have absorbed to themselves all the petty parties that sprang up four years ago and logically belong to them. During this campaign they will absorb all the other bogus parties that may yet spring up like little weeds in a forest of oaks. This development . . . has been helped along by the action of the Socialist Labor Party itself.[68]

That this was a serious misreading of the American political scene De Leon was soon to learn. It was perhaps harmless to imagine that the SLP had played much of a part in eliminating the Populists, whose merger with the Democrats in 1896 De Leon must have had chiefly in mind when he referred to petty parties absorbed by the two big ones. But it was a serious aberration to suppose that with the Republicans, the Democrats, and the SLP firmly rooted in its soil, American politics had become a densely crowded grove which could afford no room for a sturdy party of radical reform. In this view the parties of Debs and Hillquit, which were moving toward fusion by way of a united ticket in the 1900 campaign, were simply "little weeds," destined to wither in the shade of the two old parties and the SLP. But in 1900 the SLP presidential ticket received 33,382 votes—less than half the vote for the socialist unity ticket of Debs and Harriman.

The results of the 1900 election seem to have dumbfounded De Leon. *The People*—it became the *Daily People* in 1900—found no words for comment until six weeks after the election.

Then, on December 22, De Leon ran an editorial explaining what had happened to the SLP vote in 1900. That vote had grown steadily from twenty to eighty thousand between 1892 and 1898 and had now slumped to little more than it had been eight years earlier. The *Daily People's* alibi was that a radical reform party of pretended socialism had stolen the SLP's vote in 1900 as it had in 1892. The Populists in 1892 had "claimed to be Socialistic if not Socialist." Now "in 1900 the difficulties of '92 reappeared in an immensely aggravated form. . . . The political lie about Populism being Socialism could fetch only the least guarded; this year's political lie, however, about Social Democracy being Socialism was infinitely more insidious." The moral of the catastrophe was that in social as in biological phenomena "there is no growth except at the cost of infinite tests of strength."

## Theory of Revolutionary Unionism

The nascent Socialist party's swamping of the SLP in the election of 1900 affected De Leon's tactical thinking, causing him to devalue electoral activity. "The formation of the Socialist party," as he himself put it, "gave impetus to the development of the Socialist Labor Party principle . . . that the union was the essential factor in the emancipation of the working class. The Marxian motto, 'only the union can give birth to the true party of labor' became the guiding light of the SLP. The party . . . considered the ballot, however useful and necessary, a secondary consideration."[69] Devaluation of electoral activity was also for De Leon a form of criticism of the tactics which came to characterize the Socialist party. From its inception the SP, against the opposition of militant industrial unionists like Debs and Haywood, tended to treat election campaigning as the main task of the party. The gradualists of the Berger right wing and the moderate Marxist center which Hillquit headed, came to regard unions as out of bounds for concerted socialist action. They took a hostile attitude toward the IWW from 1905 onwards. By 1909 they made non-intervention in union affairs by socialists as socialists official party policy. The hope of the right and center socialists was that their neutrality in internal union affairs would help gain the party the political support of the AFL leadership.[70]

Against the background of the rival Socialist party's concentration on electoral activity and its drift toward accommodation with the AFL leadership, De Leon developed his theory of revolutionary unionism. He expounded it in *Two Pages from Roman History* (1902), *The Preamble of the IWW* (1905), and *As to Politics* (1907). His first theoretical effort was to lay down guiding lines of socialist strategy and tactics appropriate to the English-speaking world, and he performed this task in *Two Pages from Roman History*. What was needed, it seemed to him, was "knowledge of the topography of the field of action" of the class struggle in North America, Britain and the Antipodes, as well as a "knowledge of the strength, the weakness; the qualities, in short, of the forces under fire." He undertook to supply the information:

> None but the political weapon can . . . emancipate the workers and rear the Socialist Republic. And none are better aware of the fact than the Capitalist Class nor, consequently, more anxious to have the Labor forces turned from the field of independent political activity. Obviously, in the interests of the Working Class, is it to arouse them to class conscious political action. What does the Labor Leader do? From England, westward over the United States and Canada to Australia, we find the Labor Leaders solidly arrayed against the very idea.

For De Leon, the labor leader was a decisive feature of the political landscape. A "strategic post and force that buttresses capitalism," the labor leader operates "demoralizingly, disastrously upon the Working Class." He enables the bourgeoisie to continue "the work of enslaving and slowly degrading the Working Class, and, along with that, the work of debasing and ruining the country." Whether the workers would prove capable of throwing off the incubus of a conservative trade union officialdom depended on the inner qualities of the workers themselves and on an adequate appreciation of those qualities by the socialists. "The Socialist Republic depends, not upon material conditions only; it depends upon these—plus clearness of vision to assist the evolutionary process. Nor was the agency of intellect needful at any previous stage of evolution in the Class Struggle to the extent that it is needful at this, the culminating one of all." De Leon saw a need and an opportunity, and also a dire alternative. Would the revolutionary class attain the requisite consciousness? "Or is the revolutionary spark of our Age to be smothered and banked up till, as in Rome of old, it leap from the furnaces, a weapon of national suicide? In the sight of the invasion of the Philippine Islands and the horrors that are coming to light, is there any to deny that the question is a burning one?" De Leon sensed that Americans bearing the torch of civilization to Southeast Asian villages might sear their own consciences and so prepare a catastrophe for the nation. Suicidal imperialism was the alternative to socialism.

It remained to appraise the qualities of "the forces under fire" in the class struggle. This De Leon did by contrasting the proletariat to the previous underdogs of class society. The bourgeoisie had come to power only after it had acquired "ownership of the physical materials essential to their own Economic System," but the proletariat when it reached for power was characterized by "a total lack of all material economic power—a novel accomplishment to a revolutionary class, in the whole range of Class Revolutions." Ownership or the lack of property made for sharp contrasts in the political conduct of the contending classes. Property had rendered the bourgeoisie virtually impervious to corruption in its revolutionary era:

> Holding the economic power, capital, on which the feudal lords had become dependent, the bourgeoisie was safe under fire. All that was left for feudalism to maneuver with was titles. It might bestow these hollow honors, throwing them as sops to the leaders of the bourgeoisie. The bourgeois was not above "rattles and toys"; but not all such "rattles and toys" could have led the bourgeois revolution into the ground. . . . Wealth imparts strength; strength self-reliance.

The victory of a class endowed with such qualities is "almost automatic." By contrast the proletariat confronts its revolution suffering from "a weakness that, unless the requisite measures of counter-action be taken, must inevitably cause the course of history to be materially deflected." The proletariat is a force every atom of which has a stomach to fill, and, withal, a precarious ability to attend to such urgent needs. . . . At time this circumstance may be a force, but it is only a fitful force. Poverty breeds lack of self-reliance. Material insecurity suggests temporary devices. Sops and lures become captivating baits. And the one and the other are in the power of the present Ruling Class to maneuver with.[71]

Having diagnosed the weakness of the proletariat, De Leon prescribed remedial exercises to render the patient fit for a revolutionary role. The proletariat should be induced to keep away from proposals for formal improvement of the machinery of politics, for the

> modern "ballot reforms," and schemes for "referendums," "initiative," "election of Federal senators by popular vote," . . . are, in the very nature of things, so many lures to allow the revolutionary heat to radiate into vacancy. They are worse than that: they are opportunities for the usurper to prosecute his own usurpatory purposes . . . with the aid and plaudits of his victims, who imagine that they are commanding, he obeying their bidding. . . . The proletarian's chance to emerge from the bewildering woods of "Capitalist Issues" is to keep his eyes riveted upon the economic interests of his own Class—the public ownership of the land on and the tools with which to work.

To this end the workers would have to be purged of any legal or moral scruples against the expropriation of private property.

> The Proletarian Revolution marches by its own light; its acts are to be judged by the Code of Legality that itself carries in its folds, not by the standards of existing Law, which is but a reflex of existing Usurpation. Indeed, in that respect, the Proletarian Revolution shares a feature of all previous revolutions, the Capitalistic included. A new Social System brings along a new Code of Morals.

But before the new social order could arrive the workers would have to be imbued with irreverance toward the old. "The Usurper ever needs the cloak of sanctity; and therefore it is of importance to strip him bare of the cover."

To foster a sense of self-reliance in the working class De

151

Leon recommended avoidance of "all alliance with any other class in its struggles, or even skirmishes with the Capitalist Class." He reasoned that "any class the proletariat may ally itself with must, though oppressed from above, itself be a fleecers' class; in other words, must be a class whose class interests rest on the subjugation of the workers." Alliances with other classes would only deprive the proletariat of "whatever chance it had to develop and acquire" self-reliance.[72]

Everything in De Leon's prescription for an ailing working class was aimed at promoting consciousness among the workers concerning their social position and possibilities. They would have to be highly educated and organized if they were ever to carry through a revolution, never mistaking "the shadow for the substance" of socialism, always choosing "sense, not sound . . . reason, not rhetoric," never susceptible to being stampeded. "The proletarian army of emancipation cannot consist of a dumb driven herd. The very idea is a contradiction in terms." Unless the masses are addressed in straightforward language, they will not be prepared for a revolutionary role. "Pantomimes, double sense and mummery may answer the purpose of a Movement in which the proletariat acts only the role of dumb driven beast of burden" but would not serve the end of a revolutionary labor movement. The socialist organization must try to refine "the character and moral fibre of the mass"; if it failed, the American vista would be bleak. It had, De Leon estimated, taken half a millennium to make the old Roman proletariat into an utterly degenerate and destructive social force. "Would it," he asked, "in these days of electric rapidity, take 500 years to shape the proletariat of the land into another world-fagot?"[73]

But who was going to perform the tremendous educational work of delivering the American workers from the corrupting influence of conservative union officials and inspiring them with revolutionary elan? De Leon had apparently lost hope by 1902 that the STLA could perform this function. He continued to believe that in the absence of a revolutionary union, conservative leaders "would, under ordinary circumstances, naturally be chosen by the rank and file to head their political outbreaks" with predictably poor results. But "it does not follow," he now acknowledged, "*because* a certain thing is bad, *therefore* a certain other thing is the proper means to remove it."[74] As a remedy the STLA had been found wanting.

By 1904 De Leon thought that the rise and fall of unions in the flux of the class struggle presented socialists with recurring chances to shape the labor movement into an effective revolutionary force. "The union formation, with its possibilities for good," he declared, "being a natural, an instinctive move, is bound to appear and reappear, and keep on reappearing." When the labor movement was in a phase of renewing its organizations the socialists could equip it "with the proper knowledge, the proper weapon, that will save it from switching off into the pure and simple quagmire."[75] It struck De Leon and leading labor radicals outside the SLP that the American workers were entering a phase of renewal. This impression led them to found the Industrial Workers of the World in 1905. "When," De Leon wondered, "were the promises of such unionism ever more favorable and worthy of support?" And he answered, "Never before in the history of the American labor movement."[76]

De Leon was a leader of the IWW for two years. From his experience of the new movement he further elaborated his theory of revolutionary unionism, first in *The Preamble of the Industrial Workers of the World*, written in 1905, and then in *As to Politics*, a brochure which brought together a series of *Daily People* articles which had first appeared in 1906 and 1907. The *Preamble* analyzes the condition of the American working class, the function of the contract, and the complementary roles of the workers' party and the unions in the socialist revolution.

De Leon's thesis on the condition of the American working class at this time was that the workers' share of the national wealth was in decline, both in relation to the shares of other classes and absolutely. The statistics at his disposal, however, did not bear this out. They showed instead that the share of the workers in the national wealth between 1860 and 1900 hovered around one-fifth, and that the average wages of individual workers during the period registered a small gain. Since these calculations were worked out on the assumption of a stationary cost of living, De Leon concluded that a correction allowing for increased prices and deteriorating quality of goods would show a material worsening in the condition of the workers. "The reports of shoddy turned out by our factories would be incredible were they not so well authenticated," he remarked. "It is particularly the housekeeper who makes acquaintance with this fact. Inquire of any woman fifty years old today and she will be able to tell you tales on the subject." Then there was food. "There is hardly any article of food, especially food that the workingman can afford to buy, that is not adulterated, consequently, that has not deteriorated in quality. . . . Health is thereby undermined, even if life is not thereby speedily snuffed."[77] Like Thorstein Veblen he was crying in the wilderness against the decline of workmanship and planned obsolescence; like Upton Sinclair he was preparing the way for the Pure Food and Drug Act.

Contracts between employers and workers, in De Leon's view, were fraudulent. Only when the parties to a contract were peers and freemen could the document be valid. Otherwise "the thing is null, void, and of no effect; it is a badge of fraud of which he is guilty who imposes the contract upon the other." Because of their subordinate position in capitalist society, De Leon was certain that the workers could not be "of contracting mind and power with the employer." This was particularly true of individual contracts such as non-union affidavits, the yellow-dog contracts which open shop employers forced on workers. "They would not be sworn to by the workingman, but by the whip of hunger held over his head. The whip took the oath, let the whip keep it." Collective bargaining contracts were also invalid under capitalism, in De Leon's mind. The proliferation of AFL craft contracts with employers was resulting in a mounting volume of jurisdictional feuds and strike-breaking. "Union molders" are

> scabbing it upon machinists; union machinists scabbing it upon elevator men; union cigarmakers upon waiters; union waiters upon brewers; union brewers upon glucose workers; union teamsters upon carpenters; union bricklayers upon cement workers; union

soft coal miners upon hard coal miners. . . . it is not the *unorganized* scab who breaks the strikes, but the *organized craft* . . . each craft when itself involved in a strike fights heroically, when not involved demeans itself as arrant scabs . . . in fatuous reverence to "contracts"![78]

The sacredness of the contract would have to be subordinated to the principle of labor solidarity if the workers were ever to gain enough self-confidence to remake society.

The complementary roles of the workers' party and the unions in the socialist revolution were presented by De Leon as a temporary division of labor between destructive and constructive arms of the labor movement. As of 1905 he thought of the SLP as a temporary, and the IWW as a permanent, expression of the labor movement, "the constructive part . . . that outlines the mold of the future social system." The temporary political arm of the labor movement would try to take possession of the state in order to do away with it, but the revolutionary unions would seek to control the means of production for the constructive "purpose of improving and enlarging all the good that is latent in them, and that capitalism dwarfs; in short, they are to be 'taken and held' in order to save them for civilization."

From the contrasting function of the political and economic organizations of labor it followed for De Leon that the tactics of the movement on the political and economic planes would differ. The party, because of its destructive mission, could not afford to compromise with its class adversaries. The unions could be more flexible. "The economic movement may take a little at a time," he explained. "It may do so because its function is ultimately to take and hold the full plants of production and save them for the human race." In De Leon's conception of the transition from capitalism to socialism in the United States, a politics of catastrophe was combined with an economics of gradualism. It is paradoxical that he thought that his gradualist socialist unions could keep their revolutionary party from declining into reformism. "Nothing short of such an economic organization will prevent the evil," he maintained.

The work of destruction which De Leon had in mind for the

party of labor was not bloody, for he was a firm advocate of political agitation and the ballot:

> Political action raises the labor movement above the category of a "conspiracy"; it places the movement in line with the spirit of the age . . . in which the masses must themselves be intelligent actors. . . . the political movement bows to the method of civilized discussion: *it gives a chance to the peaceful solution of the great question at issue.*[79]

The chances for a peaceful solution in the United States were excellent. The best variant would have been for the revolutionary party to win a majority in a legal election, take office, immediately vest authority in the unions, and dissolve itself and all other existing political institutions. A less desirable but still acceptable variant would have occurred if the workers were robbed of electoral victory by a dishonest count. In that event authority could be assumed by the unions through a general strike or—as De Leon preferred to term it—a general lockout of the capitalist class. In either case the mission of the workers' party would have been completed once the capitalists were out of power and industry in the hands of the proletarian economic organization. There would be no justification for a proletarian dictatorship to usher in the classless, stateless society. "The political movement of labor, that, in the event of triumph would prolong its existence a second after triumph, would be a usurpation."

All this rested on De Leon's assumption that the United States was the most civilized country in the world, and that the American capitalists would not make a violent stand for their wealth and power. The organized and enlightened American workers, he conjectured, would simply cow their bosses. To support this view he drew contrasting character sketches of the European and the American ruling classes. In Europe the feudal spirit still prevailed, even permeating the bourgeoisie. A man reared in the feudal tradition was brave and combative. "Valor is the burden of the songs that rock his cradle; valor is the theme of the nursery tales to which he is raised; deeds of valor are the ideals set up before him." Wilhelm II of Germany, "semi-crippled, semi-crazy," personified the European ruling classes. "He will fight whatever the odds." Hence there would be no peaceful transition to socialism in Europe. Power and wealth were held by a different sort of men in the United States.

Was it songs of valor that rocked the cradles of our capitalist rulers? Was it tales of noble daring that formed the theme of the nursery tales to which they were brought up? Were the ideals that they gathered from their home surroundings the ideals of manliness? No! Daily experience, confirmed by every investigation that one set of capitalists institutes against another, tells us that they reached their present status of rulers by putting sand into your sugar, by watering their stocks, by putting shoddy into your clothes, by pouring water into your molasses, by breaches of trust, by fraudulent failures and fraudulent fires, in short by *swindle*. (Applause). Now, then, the swindler is a coward. Like a coward, he will play the bully, as we see the capitalist class doing, toward the weak, the weak because disorganized working class. Before the strong, the bully crawls.[80]

De Leon's hope for a peaceful transition in America, then, depended on the assumption that a parvenu oligarchy would defend its ill-gotten gains with less determination than would a long-established ruling class its "legitimate" stake in society. He hoped that the American bourgeoisie of his generation was so nurtured in the spirit of rugged individualism as to be incapable of acts of individual self-sacrifice in behalf of their class: they would meet a social crisis not with the values of Roland but with the values of Falstaff and Horatio Alger. Whatever the inaccuracies of this moral portrait of America's men of wealth and power, it is undeniable that with the growth of labor organization since De Leon's time the violent bullying of American workers by their employers has markedly diminished. It has been a long time since Pullman and Homestead and Cripple Creek, and even since the Little Steel Strike of 1937.

When De Leon prepared his lecture on *The Preamble of the IWW* in 1905 his influence in the new industrial union was waxing. He had played a large part in formulating the principles of the organization. Subsequently he headed with William E. Trautmann and Vincent St. John the IWW's dominant revolutionary wing. Trautmann and St. John were not De Leonists. They agreed with De Leon only on the need for a revolutionary union; they saw no need for socialist political action: they were American anarcho-syndicalists. In the IWW's first year the De Leon-Trautmann-St. John combination held together in common hostility to Charles O. Sherman, first and only president of the IWW. Sherman, though an industrial unionist, was no revolutionary. The revolutionaries ousted him and abolished his office at the IWW's second convention in 1906. After that the combination of Marxists led by De Leon, and anarcho-syndicalists led by Trautmann and St. John, came apart and the influence of De Leon within the IWW began to wane. At the 1906 convention it was settled that the IWW would remain a revolutionary union. It remained to be settled whether the IWW would be a Marxist or an anarcho-syndicalist union. Two more years were required to settle that issue. In 1908 De Leon and his followers were excluded from the IWW and the "anti-politicals" under St. John assumed undisputed control.[81]

During the waning of his influence in the IWW De Leon wrote *As to Politics*. The pamphlet is a dialogue between anarcho-syndicalist readers of the *Daily People* and De Leon. Under the influence of De Leon in 1905 the IWW had held that the workers must "come together on the political, as well as on the industrial field, and take and hold that which they produce by their labor through an economic organization of the working class, without affiliation to any political party."[82] The anarcho-syndicalists did not like this formula, and in November 1906 De Leon opened the columns of his paper to correspondence on whether the "political clause" should be kept in the IWW's declaration of principles. De Leon and his critics argued the question in print for four months.

The dialogue evoked varied objections to political action. One of De Leon's critics, John Sandgren, doubted that the working class constituted a majority of the American electorate but granted for the sake of argument that it did. Could that "problematical working class majority" be rallied to a revolutionary program "in any reasonable time?"

Probably not. The ruling class holds the strings of bread and butter of millions of slaves so tightly that they can not vote for revolution. Furthermore, the ruling class controls the schools and poisons the minds of the children. It owns the press and controls the minds of the full-grown. It controls the pulpit, and there pollutes the mind of child and man. What becomes of your working class majority before these facts?

In reply to this argument from mass society De Leon acknowledged that bourgeois influences "no doubt must be reckoned with." But, he pointed out,

if these influences are so absolutely controlling that these wage slaves will be too timid to perform such a task as voting [for the revolution] . . . upon what ground can the writer feel justified to enroll those same slaves as reliable material for the revolutionary act of the I.W.W.? If they must be excluded from the former they can not for a moment be thought of for the latter.[83]

Sandgren also argued against participation in elections on the grounds that a total of eighteen million minors, women, foreigners, Negroes and migratory workers "can in no manner be directly interested in politics." This total was likely to increase, since there was no "reasonable justification for hoping that the master class will cease to impose new restrictions upon the right to vote, when that has been their course for the last ten years, as witness Texas, Louisiana, Mississippi, Georgia, North Carolina, Virginia and other states." De Leon's rejoinder was that

all, except the infants and the sick can be made carriers of the educational and agitational propaganda of the revolution conducted upon the civilized plane. Though they be not entitled to cast a single vote, they can distribute literature, and those who have the gift—though foreign, female, Negro or otherwise disfranchised— can by speech promote the revolution by teaching it on the political platform.[84]

It was further objected by Sandgren that if socialists won state elections they would disgrace themselves, for socialist governors and legislatures would be unable to build the socialist commonwealth in a single state and would necessarily limit themselves to reform tinkering with the capitalist structure. "To do anything else would bring upon them the U.S. Supreme Court and eventually the U.S. regular troops." To this De Leon found no easy response. "The value of the 'ballot' as a constructive force," he conceded, "is zero."[85] Pressed further on this point he admitted that a revolutionary crisis could occur in the United States before the workers had had an opportunity to win elections. He sketched a possible course of events:

> A strike will break out; capitalist brutality will cause the strike to spread; physical besides moral support will pour forth from other not immediately concerned branches of the Working Class. A condition of things—economic, political, social-atmospheric—will set in, akin to the condition of things in 1902, at the time of the great coal miners' strike, or in 1894, at at the time of the Pullman-A.R.U. strike. What then? The issue will depend wholly upon the degree, in point of quality and in point of quantity, that the organization of the I.W.W. will have reached.

If the revolutionary union was strong enough, then the "class instinct that Marx teaches the Socialist to rely on . . . will readily crystallize around" it. "Further efforts for a peaceful measuring of strength would then have been rendered superfluous by capitalist barbarism. Capitalism would be swept aside forthwith."[86]

Here De Leon went as far in conciliating his anarcho-syndicalist critics as he could go and still be an advocate of political action. But he could not satisfy critics who were demanding discontinuance of political action not in some future eventuality but then and there. This was beyond De Leon, convinced as he was that without political action "the emancipation of the workers would be indefinitely postponed, and could then be reached only by wading through a massacre, both the delay and the then assuredly vast amount of bloodshed being brought on and rendered necessary by the workers themselves." For De Leon political action was educational: the more political action, the more consciousness; the more consciousness, the less violence.

Some of De Leon's critics in the IWW thought that political

action was superfluous because civil war between capitalists and workers had already broken out in the United States. "The capitalist class," declared Sandgren,

has already chosen war. Our blood has run in torrents, as in the Paris Commune, or bespattered the road to Hazelton and Cripple Creek; the rope has strangled some of our early champions and is in preparation for others. . . . The war has been going on these many years and is raging fiercely now. How can anybody suggest a peaceable settlement, especially when we demand a complete surrender?

"If we are in a state of war," asserted V. H. Kopald, "then war is hell and civilization is impossible. . . . Civilized agitation between victims and bandits! Nonsense!" "Do we really live in a constitutional country," wondered O. Eherich, "or is it only an illusion?"[87]

In answer De Leon drew attention to two separate meanings of war which his critics had muddled. The class war was going on all the time, he acknowledged. But "war, in the sense used by Sandgren, has not yet broken out. If it had, his articles could not be published in *The People*, this discussion could not be going on, the capitalist institutions would not be available for the transportation of our thoughts, and neither could write with the peace and comfort that we do."

De Leon's effort to get his critics to see that the United States was not in a civil war was hamstrung by an act of audacious violence initiated by the governors of Colorado and Idaho. Early in 1906 two leaders and a friend of the Western Federation of Miners were arrested in Denver, put aboard a special train and carried—without a chance to seek a stay of extradition—to Boise to stand trial for the murder of Frank Stuenenberg, a former Governor of Idaho. The sense of outrage which gripped labor radicals during the trial of William D. Haywood, Charles Moyer, and George Pettibone is conveyed by an article Debs wrote for the *Appeal to Reason* of March 10, 1906:

Nearly twenty years ago the capitalist tyrants put some innocent men to death for standing up for labor.

They are now going to try it again. Let them dare! There have been twenty years of revolutionary education, agitation, and organization since the Haymarket tragedy, and if an attempt is made to repeat it, there will be a revolution and I will do all in my power to precipitate it. . . .

If they attempt to murder Moyer, Haywood and their brothers, a million revolutionists at least will meet them with their guns.

It was with the abduction and trial of Haywood, Moyer, and Pettibone in mind that Eherich had asked De Leon whether "we really live in a constitutional country." De Leon replied that

the capitalist class has violated the constitution in the instance of the Colorado men. But that is not evidence enough of the existence of actual war. The rest of us are doing what Haywood was kidnapped for, and yet we are at large. The kidnapping and other outrages had taken place, and yet the convention of the Industrial Workers of the World met and worked in peace.[88]

De Leon had the better of the argument yet his reasoning failed to persuade. His logical triumphs accompanied dwindling influence in the IWW. He must have sensed that while winning the debate he was losing the struggle, for in his final contribution to the dialogue in *As to Politics* he cast a dark look into the American future and had a vision of mass society:

The downfall of capitalism . . . is by no means equivalent with the uprise of the Socialist Republic. . . . The country is now moving into a social system to which the name "Capitalism," in its proper sense, is applying less and less. A monopoly period is now surging upward to which the designation "Plutocratic Feudalism" is a fitter term. It does not follow that, if the very Few are gathered on one side, and very Many are lumped on the other, the latter will necessarily swamp the former. They will do so only when they shall have understood their own revolutionary mission, and organized accordingly. Contrariwise—let the Working Class continue a sufficiently longer spell befuddled . . . then, whatever periods of senseless (senseless because unrevolutionary and therefore, merely riotous) upheavals may betide, the Many will sink to the depths of serfs, actual serfs of a plutocratic feudal glebe.[89]

TOWARD A NEW THEORY OF SOCIALIST ORGANIZATION

The vision of "plutocratic feudalism" spurred De Leon to seek anew a path to a different and better future for America. The rapid growth of a Socialist party in which he had no faith and the turn of the IWW away from Marxism towards anarcho-syndicalism showed De Leon that American politics would not flow in the course he had charted for it in 1899 when he proclaimed that the SLP had become "a Party indeed." He now began to project a new party of socialism which would replace the SLP and the SP.

Initially De Leon thought that the new party should be a larger edition of the SLP. "What the name of that political party will be it is now too early to know," he wrote in *As to Politics.* "What the leading characteristics of that Party will be—*that* is knowable today." It would be a homogeneous party rather than a confederation of regional and ideological groupings like the Socialist party—"*one* thing only to all men, *one* thing in all latitudes and longitudes of the land—no perfidy to principle under the guise of 'autonomy.'" It would not be limited to actual wage workers but "must have room within its camp for all desirable social elements whose occupation excludes them from bona fide membership in the Industrial Workers of the World." It would accept the IWW as "the embryo of future society."[90]

The new party would differ from the SLP in one way: it would need a new leader whose lustre was undimmed by involvement in the internecine conflicts of the radicals, and whose authority derived from his participation in the class battles of the day. Following Haywood's acquittal in the Boise trial De Leon wrote to him on August 3, 1907 to suggest that his "celebrated case" had prepared him "for the work of unifying the movement on solid ground." He knew that "those who have been early in the struggle" like himself and his SLP comrades had "necessarily drawn upon themselves animosities" which disqualified them as the sponsors of socialist unity. On this score De Leon was nothing if not self-effacing: he knew that he was not the man for the moment. The American political situation of the moment reminded him of the eighteen-fifties. "We are now again," he told Haywood, "in the days when the old Republican party was organized out of the warring free-soil and abolitionist, and up to then wavering elements."

Haywood left De Leon's letter unanswered. The animosities to which De Leon had referred were indeed deep. To Haywood De Leon seemed not only unfit to initiate unification but even to participate in a socialist unity arranged by others. Haywood was certain that De Leon would make it "impossible for any except his devotees to work with him" and that an SLP "dominated by De Leon's prejudices . . . could not lend strength to any movement with which it became associated."[91]

Until 1908 De Leon thought that a homogeneous revolutionary party was an immediate need in the United States. That is what he meant when he wrote to Haywood about "unifying the movement on solid ground." But with the failure of his overture to Haywood and the rout of the Marxists in the IWW he thoroughly revised his view of the appropriate form of socialist organization for America. He put forward his new view in a lecture given in New York on February 21, 1908.

De Leon now took the Second International as his model. It had fraternally united a broad spectrum of tendencies "from the most rudimentary, like Zionist-Socialism, up to the most clearly and soundly revolutionary, like the Socialist Labor Party—provided they all aim, remotely or approximately, mediately or immediately, at the overthrow of the capitalist system of production." The all-inclusiveness of the International was a good thing. "The International Congress takes in the 'Mountain' and the 'Vale,' leaving to time to demonstrate whether the 'impossibilist' 'Mountain' of to-day, or the 'possibilist' Vale is to be the force of tomorrow." The tolerance of the world movement, thought De Leon, set the warring socialist parties of the United States a good example. "The theory of the International Congress regarding the 'Socialist family' establishes the broad basis of concerted action. The application of the theory by the International Congress— proportional representation and freedom of agitational methods— points the way for the same application in America."

To bring together the revolutionaries and reformists of America in a single party, De Leon suggested, would require no abandoning of principle on either side but only the recognition by each that the other was performing a useful function: this much "the 'Vale' must, by experience, be ready to concede to the 'Mountain,' and, inversely, the 'Mountain' to the 'Vale.' " In saying this De Leon admitted what he had adamantly denied since he had become a Marxist—the legitimacy of a reformist socialist movement in the United States. While conceding this he reiterated that most or all of the SLP program would be applicable "when the Movement turns the lap of the 'home-stretch.' " But, he cautioned, "essential to the ultimate success of a Revolutionary Movement as may be and is the upholding, constant and clear to view, of all the means necessary *on the day* of the 'home-stretch,' just so necessary may, *before that day*, and simultaneously, be the looser methods of the 'Vale.' " The earlier De Leon had posed the dilemma: reform or revolution? He was now ready to respond: reform *and* revolution. No other response was suitable in a country where "primitive opportunities" for enrichment "still occasionally crop up even in regions where capitalism is strongest" and where "diversity of conditions" were "reflected in a variety of mental stages of development."

De Leon now saw that the Socialist party which he had fought since its birth was a more characteristic expression of America than was the SLP. He saw no more justification for an independent Marxist party in the United States of 1908 than Marx and Engels had seen for one in the Germany of 1847.[92] No more did he inveigh against the autonomy-minded SP violating the principle that a true party of socialism "must be *one* thing only to all men, *one* thing in all latitudes and longitudes of the land." Instead De Leon wanted a unification between the SP and the SLP wherein "mutual criticism would continue—sharp, if you please, but [with] the harshness of the manner . . . chastened to the profit of the matter."[93]

De Leon's rethinking of the theory of party organization was courageous but badly timed. It was ironical that at the moment when De Leon was beginning to look favorably on an all-inclusive socialist party, the SP under the control of Berger and Hillquit was losing its diversity and tending toward homogeneity. There was small chance that an SP leadership which tried to replace Debs with a more moderate presidential candidate in 1908 would have welcomed the De Leonists.[94] Nor would the left opposition to the leadership led by Haywood. In the SLP there was great reluctance to unite with the SP. Henry Kuhn, De Leon's right hand in the SLP, opposed the idea. "If we of the S.L.P. permit the further existence of our movement to be continually called in question," he argued, "we simply weaken and injure our movement . . . We show a lack of faith in the correctness of our position."[95] Even for a leader with the authority of De Leon it would have been a difficult feat to have induced the SLP to have renounced its congenital hostility to the SP. When he spoke out for unity he had to say that "I do not stand here in my official capacity in the Party and not even as a Party member. I speak here simply as one of the many people active in the Socialist Movement, and merely exercising the right of thought and speech."[96] Whether because the SP leaders showed no interest, or for some other reason, De Leon did not press his view of unity on his party.

With unity a dead issue the political evolution of the SLP was virtually complete. De Leonism was a finished system. The evolution was fateful and the system impressive. Had De Leon never lived, American radicalism in his own time and in later decades would have been different than it was—for better and for worse. If the chroniclers have been less than generous with De Leon, it is because fortune dealt so severely with his attempt to build a movement. The defeated are usually seen through the eyes of the victors.

### De Leon and the Tradition

Relating De Leonist Marxism to the American radical tradition is most easily accomplished by noticing De Leon's view of the American Revolution and of the movements for ethnic and sexual equality. De Leon celebrated the American Revolution as a victory in mankind's struggle toward social equality. The revolution, he insisted, had been made by generous-spirited men who took the Declaration of Independence seriously. They were moved by a libertarian ardor unmatched in their French contemporaries. The revolutionary French bourgeoisie used the slogan of equality knowing that it concealed the social reality that hereditary classes would persist after their revolution. "Our revolutions, on the contrary, really imagined that the heart and the mind were abreast of each other. . . . they could not conceive of such a thing as wage workers by extraction." They could not know that "Property, the light thing that was to give freedom," would become "the weapon of oppression. We cannot blame them . . . And if Franklin lived today and the revolutionary fathers, they would realize that what they imagined would be the means of freedom had become the means of oppression."[97]

De Leon's respect for the makers of the American Revolution led him to protest the debunking of the founding fathers by economic determinist historians like A. M. Simons and Charles Beard. Had all the talk of life, liberty, and the pursuit of happiness been only a facade for bourgeois self-seeking? Only "dry-as-dust dogmatists, whose Socialism goes by rote" would think so. They thought the egalitarian rhetoric of the revolutionists hypocritical because the revolutionists failed to eliminate property qualifications for voting and to abolish slavery. These failures, thought De Leon, do not "detract from the genuineness of the revolutionary spirit of 1776" since property was widely distributed and slavery was "not then the national institution it developed into later." The debunkers "deprive the gorgeous Morgan-Marx theory . . . of much splendor, incisiveness and many-sided luminousness by denying the Revolutionary Fathers of America all sincerity in their fervid proclamations of freedom." Historical materialism indeed "receives marked demonstration from the sincere, however fatuous, belief of the Revolutionary Fathers that they had established freedom on permanent foundations."[98]

In defending the leaders of the Revolution De Leon did not wish to seem the patronizing modern. The Declaration of Independence was "no idiot's work." It was "the product of the Age's experience and learning, coupled with the virgin conditions in the land" and it opened a new page in social polity. Thereafter "collective society in America assumed the duty of guaranteeing to the individual a free field—EQUALITY OF OPPORTUNITIES." That duty has been shirked, yet the ideal of equal opportunities remains "a vital force, propelling socialism."[99] Socialism would achieve the deferred promise of the American Revolution by fulfilling the historic movements toward social democracy of Negroes, women, and the working class.

De Leon viewed the Negro struggle as an aspect of the class struggle. Like all American Marxists of his time, including Debs, he did not see it as an independent movement of social radicalism.[100] He failed to revise Marx's precipitous conclusion that "as the American War of Independence initiated a new era of ascendency for the middle class, so the American anti-slavery war will do for the working classes."[101] To expect that the Civil War would end the Negro's degradation and place labor's emancipation on the American agenda was the optimism of 1864. Among American Marxists it did not wear off until after World War I and the Russian Revolution. De Leon knew that Negroes were losing the vote in the South in the nineties, but he saw disfranchisement less as an occasion to agitate for Negro rights than as a stick to beat the Populists and Silver Democrats out of their radical pretensions. When Pitchfork Ben Tillman thundered in the Senate for free silver in 1896, *The People* scored him for disenfranchising Negroes and propertyless whites and drew the moral that "the loudest declaimers on behalf of the 'toiling masses' and denouncers of the monopolists are often the working class's most firmly set tyrants, whose rage at the monopolists does not proceed from a sense of justice but from anger at being outdone at their own rascality."[102]

In 1908 De Leon still regarded the plight of the Negro as essentially a class issue. White supremacy, he thought, was only the pretended motive of the southern drive against Negro civil rights. The "pretense" was "transparent" to him. "The tanglefoot Suffrage legislation while aimed at the Negro ostensibly as a Negro, in fact aims at him as a wage slave."[103] It was a waste of time for socialists to explore the differences between whites and blacks. "More difficult, withal useful to the Movement, is the discovery of that which may be identical in all—their proletarian character. This is the creative discovery." He saw nothing at all creative in the attitude of those to the right of him in the movement toward race and the related question of immigration.

A resolution on immigration had been debated at the Amsterdam Congress which had the backing of Hillquit, Schlueter, and Algernon Lee of the American Socialist party, as well as of Dutch and Australian socialists. The proposed resolution was a bad omen for the future of the International. It opposed immigration into developed countries of "workingmen of inferior races (Chinese, Negroes, etc.)" and charged that such "cheap labor" was "a willing object of exploitation." De Leon attacked the racism of the resolution. "Where," he asked, "is the line that separates the 'inferior' from the 'superior' races?" What kind of men were those socialists who were prepared to consign a portion of humanity to the category of "etc."? The international movement might find a warning in the American experience of xenophobia. "To the native American proletariat, the Irish were made to appear an 'inferior' race; to the Irish, the German; to the German, the Italian; to the Italian—and so on down the line through the Swedes, the Poles, the Jews, the Armenians, the Japanese, to the end of the gamut. Socialism knows not such insulting, iniquitous distinctions as 'inferior' and 'superior' races among the proletariat. It is for capitalism to fan the fires of such sentiments in its scheme to keep the proletariat divided."[104] This attack produced a verbal change of dubious value. The proponents of the resolution dropped "inferior" from the text, replacing it with "backward." But they persisted in their opposition to the immigration of "Chinese, Negroes, etc."

De Leon saw more revolutionary potential in the feminist movement than in the movements of Negroes and other races and nationalities struggling for equality. Attacking the wrongs done woman, he observed in 1903, that this oppression

> touches a nerve that aches from end to end of the capitalist world. There is no woman, whatever her station, but in one way or another is a sufferer, a victim of modern society. . . . Accordingly,

the invocation of the "Rights of Woman" not only arouses the spirit of the heaviest sufferers under capitalist society and thereby adds swing to the blows of the male militants in their efforts to overthrow the existing order, it also lames the adversary by raising sympathizers in his own camp, and inciting sedition among his own retinue.[105]

Woman suffrage was praised by De Leon as a movement possessed of a "dignity and import" which could belong to no mere reform. The suffragists, however, were to be censured for being "blind to the origin and development of classes; blind, accordingly" to the relation between their cause and "the great Social Question of our generation." He warned them that "a Social Movement can not, in these days, remain neutral in the issue between the Proletariat and the Capitalist Class." If they failed to make a revolutionary alliance with labor, they probably would not gain their point, for the trend since the nineties had been towards an ever-narrower franchise. Jim Crow legislation could well be the prelude to a nation-wide restoration of property qualifications for voting. But if, contrary to his expectation, women gained the vote under capitalism, it would mean that the guardians of the status quo had discounted the revolutionary impulse in the twentieth-century suffrage movement and were showing "an even greater contempt for the woman wage slave" than for the man.[106] De Leon knew that the early labor movement had regarded male suffrage as "a sort of miraculous weapon, instinct with power to perform wonders" and that having striven for the vote "to the neglect of all other things," they had found suffrage to be "an alphabet, with which bad as well as good words can be spelled."[107] If he expected a happier result from the woman suffrage movement, it was on the condition that the movement not neglect other issues.

For De Leon the hope of movements of racial and sexual equality lay in their integration with the labor movement. "One thing at a time," he suggested, "may or may not be easier to secure than a whole lot. That depends. . . . Where the thing to be secured is part of an organic whole, then the one-at-a-time theory is an optical illusion." Here De Leon spoke with the accents of

Brownson's "typical Yankee" radical who had engaged himself simultaneously in peace, temperance, abolition, and women's rights proceedings. He was led to express himself in this way by his sense of the revolutionary nature of his age, for only an age of revolution demands an organic approach to politics. He readily acknowledged that if he were wrong about the nature of the age, he was also wrong to advocate amalgamating the movements of social radicalism. The one-at-a-time tactic of the suffragists was legitimate if "the demand of Woman for the ballot, at this season, is a reform." Had he felt his age to be reformist rather than revolutionary, De Leon might have followed Brownson in blinking at one social wrong in order to concentrate on rectifying another. But De Leon was sure that was a false course in twentieth-century America. "At revolutionary periods the blinking at one Wrong extenuates the Wrong protested against: it is a feature of revolutionary periods that kindred Wrongs, all the Wrongs rooted in a central Wrong that the revolution is up in arms against, are blended into one, and are jointly attacked."[108] De Leon was here in the tradition of Jefferson who in 1780 had seen the revolution as the occasion for a broad assault on several political and social evils which could be less easily dealt with in calmer times: "the shackles, therefore, which shall not be knocked off at the conclusion of this war, will remain on us long, will be made heavier and heavier, till our rights shall revive or expire in a convulsion."[109]

De Leon believed he lived in a time when political greatness was within the reach of mankind, when a synthesis rarely observed in history was possible—the harmony of morality and politics:

For generations people have been singing the psalms of the Psalmist and doing the acts of fiends; preaching the admonitions of the Prophets and indulging in the ways of the wicked; professing Christianity and practicing deviltry. The days of this generation promise to end the hypocrisy. A keener spirit, awakened by fuller knowledge, is rising to demand of man that he practice what he preaches . . . insisting that he do so at the cost of being whipped out of the temple of humanity that he desecrates with his criminal conduct.

Whatever reason may or may not have been at one time for looking upon the maxim "Do unto others as you would have others do unto you" as beyond human reach, that time has passed."[110]

In this faith De Leon was at one with traditional American radicalism.

☆☆☆ *Chapter 6*


# Perspectives


For almost ninety years the voices of Brownson, Weydemeyer, Sorge, and De Leon were representative of labor radicalism in the United States. Each shared with his successors a part of his thought and practice, and the thought and practice of each was repudiated in part by his successors. Together they accumulated a tradition which was received in large measure by the Socialist party in the time of Debs and in very small measure by the Communist party of Foster and Browder. It is the aim here to summarize the heritage of American labor radicalism from Brownson through De Leon, and to see how it was accepted or repudiated by the organized labor radicalisms of the twentieth century. The essense of the heritage is disclosed by comparing what Brownson, Weydemeyer, Sorge, and De Leon thought about several American historical, social, and political issues. These issues are the significance of the American Revolution; the tempo of social change in America; the relation of labor radicalism to other social radicalisms; popular acceptance of private property and religion; popular fear of violence in social change; and finally, the proper description of the condition of the American working class. For Brownson, Europe was the source of revolutionary theory and the United States the locale of revolutionary action. American social democratic movements, he thought, would fulfil the egalitarian promise of the American Revolution. Weydemeyer, when he formed the American Workers League in 1853, accepted Brownson's view of the revolution. Under Sorge the German-American Marxists dropped appeals to the American Revolutionary tradition. As leader of the International and member of the National Labor Union and International Labor Union, Sorge was not trying to reach the public at large with a message of political action but only the wage workers with a message of organization. Regarding the Anglo-Saxons as the least important strain in the American working class of his time, he may have felt no need to allude to the native radical tradition. The circumstance that the followers of Sylvis in the National Labor Union and the followers of Andrews in the International appealed to the native tradition, probably inhibited Sorge from trying to relate Marxism to the tradition.

Among the Marxists the idea of labor radicalism as a movement to redeem the promise of the American Revolution came back into vogue at the end of the eighties. The SLP in 1889 adopted a new program reasserting "the inalienable right of all men to life, liberty and the pursuit of happiness," and holding "with the founders of the American Republic . . . that the purpose of government is to secure every citizen in the enjoyment of this right."[1] De Leon himself expounded this theme throughout his career as a Marxist. His presentation of it differed from Brownson's. Brownson thought that the social radicalisms would achieve their ends one at a time but De Leon favored simultaneous attacks on various forms of oppression. This divergence in tactics reflected a difference between Brownson and De Leon over the American tempo of social change.

Brownson took the long view that the emancipation of labor might well be accomplished by a later generation than his own, but De Leon lived in the conviction that America was on the verge of revolution. Weydemeyer did not live long enough after the Civil War to have to grapple with the problem of the American rate of change, but Sorge came to agree with Brownson that the tempo would be slow and the method would be to work on one issue at a time. In contrast, De Leon revived the organic approach to politics of the transcendental radicals against which Brownson had set his face in the eighteen-thirties and Sorge in the eighteen-seventies. In De Leon the organic approach was manifested in his simultaneous efforts to organize industrial unions and conduct socialist political campaigns, as well as in the high value he put on the woman suffrage movement.

De Leon understood the logical connection between the way a politician views his age and the political tactics he adopts. For him an organic politics was in resonance with a revolutionary age, while an orderly concentration on one objective at a time was better suited to an age of evolutionary gradualism. Though De Leon's appraisal of his age led him to reject the one-at-a-time tactic, the distinction he drew between the destructive role of socialist politics and the constructive role of socialist unionism allowed him to sanction a gradual movement of socialist unions toward control of the economy. Late in life De Leon acknowledged that the reformist character of American labor politics would not be quickly outlived, but he kept faith in the approach of a revolution which would demand comprehensive solidarity among the movements of social radicalism. As he conceived of it, the principle of solidarity was incompatible with one-at-a-time attacks on social evils, for solidarity and subordination did not go together. De Leon would not say with Sorge that woman suffrage was meaningless without the labor revolution; what he did say about it was that it was unobtainable without unity between the feminists and the labor radicals.

Sensitivity to American public opinion was revealed by the four labor radicals in what they said about private property, religion, and the use of violence. The property question split the Workingmen's party of New York in 1828, the year that Brownson joined it. The Thomas Skidmore faction of the Workingmen demanded confiscation of the property of the rich. The Robert Dale Owen-Frances Wright faction of the Workingmen opposed the Skidmore demand.[2] Brownson at the time sided with Owen and Wright, but a dozen years later he advocated a modified form of Skidmore's demand when he proposed abolition of the right of inheritance. Flaunting this proposal in the face of a public partial to the idea of property, Brownson took the stand that he was not going to be cowed into silence for the sake of expediency and party regularity. Still, he tried to mollify outraged feelings with the assurance that he raised the idea only for discussion and that "its realization is far distant in the future."[3]

Sorge showed more concern for public opinion about property than Brownson. In 1876 Sorge went as far, if not farther, toward repudiating the idea of confiscation as any socialist had ever gone. Sorge promised that socialists would take nothing from the rich but would merely prevent them from using their fortunes to further enrich themselves. De Leon showed no concern for sentiment in favor of private property. He quoted Skidmore with approval on the justice of confiscating the wealth of the capitalists.

Sorge had agitated against religion for at least fifteen years before he became a Marxist. Subsequently, he was not troubled by the danger that socialism might suffer by association with ir-religion. Brownson, by contrast, became convinced after 1830 that socialism could have no American future if it failed to divest itself of Owenite rationalism and find support in the Gospels. De Leon was sure that "from a scientific point of view, the Fall of Man is an idle nursery tale; from the moral point of view it is a slander on the race."[4] But De Leon feared that a bellicose atheism would needlessly deprive socialism of the sympathy of the religious-minded. When he translated Bebel, De Leon cushioned for American readers the German socialist's thrusts at religion.[5]

Sorge and De Leon seemed more sensitive to popular fear of violence than was Brownson. Sorge advocated a humane and orderly evolution to socialism, and De Leon urged bowing to the civilized method of settling disputes. But Brownson prophesied the coming world revolution in an apocalyptic voice:

> If a general war should break out, it will involve all quarters of the globe, and it will be in the end more than a war between nations.

It will resolve itself into a social war, a war between two social elements; between the aristocracy and the democracy, between the people and their masters. It will be a terrible war![6]

Brownson knew in 1840 that the material condition of the American workers had improved since the revolution. But he asserted that the relative position of the workers in American society had not improved at all and that their attempts to keep abreast of the national style of life would become more and more desperate. The documents of the Marxists led by Weydemeyer and Sorge contain nothing so sophisticated as this. The platform of Weydemeyer's American Workers League speaks of the daily worsening of the condition of the workers while Sorge's branch of the NLU declared that unions had been unsuccessful in bettering the condition of the workers.

Only with De Leon did American Marxism arrive at an appreciation of the condition of the workers as subtle as Brownson's. De Leon's description reduces it to three elements. The first is a long view of the history of human needs:

The savage ancestors of the human race needed but their nails to grub food with, and satisfy their aspirations; their barbarian successors began to use tools, bows and arrows, and to require skins of animals for clothing; their still more advanced descendants needed pottery, then fixed fields for agriculture, then fortified towns; today, we, the latest scions in the long line of descent, have needs unknown to these ancestors, aspirations of which they had no inkling. . . . Every usurping class, from the remotest times down to the present, that withheld or withholds from the laborer that whereby he lived or lives, has successively had to face the music of the "wild men's talk." . . . It has regularly been the knell of their reign.[7]

The second element is to show that the sense of misery and the standard of living are independent variables:

In all likelihood, the Hottentot suffers less than the Russian peasant; the Russian peasant less than the workers in the German Empire; the workers in the German Empire less than their fellow proletarians of Great Britain; the proletariat of Great Britain less than their fellows in the United States.

De Leon was not indulging himself here in the cult of the primitive for he readily admitted that the American workers were better off than others. But for De Leon the superiority of their condition consisted chiefly in the circumstance that the American workers had "a nearer and better opportunity to cast off all social suffering." If American workers suffered more than workers and peasants and tribesmen of other societies, it was only because the Americans sensed they were "within reach of actual freedom."[8] In this, De Leon's view of the quality of American workingclass life is close to Brownson's, for Brownson also considered wage labor to be the most miserable of exploitative relationships. For Brownson, too, the superiority of the condition of the American workers consisted solely in their nearness to total freedom.

The third element in De Leon's appreciation of the condition of the working class goes beyond Brownson, who thought that radical discontent would persist because the workers would never catch up with the national style of life. De Leon concluded that the workers' needs might be met under capitalism in a stultifying way. Conceding that "the capitalist class is not always reckless of the two-legged cattle which, together with the four-legged ones, are needed for production," De Leon suggested that an idea might strike "the minds of the employing class to the effect that a well-fed, well housed and musically entertained wage slave yields more wool than an under-fed, badly housed and unentertained one."[9] For De Leon the disintegration of the labor movement in a mass society was a frightening alternative to the socialist revolution.

### Appraisals of the Four Leaders

Despite the determined and intelligent work of Brownson, Weydemeyer, Sorge, and De Leon labor radicalism did not become a mass movement in the United States. Their failure has been judged in various ways by their continuators. Isaac T. Hecker, who had worked with Brownson in the Workingmen's party and later founded the Paulist Fathers, thought that a great movement might have been started by Brownson if only he had remained a radical after he became a Catholic. Brownson's apostasy from radicalism cut him off from the Yankee transcendentalists. "The best minds of New England," writes Hecker, "were ripe for the study of the essential truths of Catholicity." But Brownson took a conservative tack "better calculated . . . to strengthen the convictions of those in the church than to attract others to her fold."[10]

Appraising the role of Weydemeyer, Sorge concluded that the American Workers League was premature. The effort "to abolish the old spirit world, to root out the traditional ideas of an earlier generation, was not yet timely in the fifties." A mysterious American "alchemy" had maintained the fluidity of the class structure and had "prevented the distillation of a chemically pure product."[11]

Sorge's activity as a Marxist has been appraised by Schlueter and, indirectly, by De Leon. Schlueter was dismayed by the lack of continuity between the International and the SLP. Schlueter thought that native American radicals of the Andrews type were partly responsible for the discontinuity. "How far these bourgeois reformers warped the struggle of the American workers towards a one-sided reliance on union activity to better their condition cannot be determined; but their reformism certainly has to answer for the enduring one-sidedness of the American labor movement." Schlueter thought the lack of influence of the old Internationalists in the SLP was also partly due to the personality of Sorge. To Schlueter, Sorge was a *Kampfnatur*. "He had a stiffness and knottiness of character which could not countenance doing things by halves and which was not given to horse-trading; his disposition made him many enemies, provoking antagonism and discord in the movement which a more accommodating man might have avoided for the sake of the cause."[12]

Appraising the fate of the International in America, De Leon did not consider the personality of the radicals to have been a notable factor in the failure of labor radicalism in Sorge's period:

> The seed of modern Socialism was first planted in American soil by German militants a generation ago. . . . there was here in those

days no "labor movement" in the true meaning which a class-conscious proletarian attaches to this expression. . . . Individualism of the meanest sort was rampant; solidarity was an unknown word. . . . The six years' crisis that began in 1873, by reducing the American working class to a condition of helplessness sufficiently suggestive of its inexorable fate under capitalism, gave the German comrades, chiefly in New York City, their first opportunity of agitation among people of other nationalities. They improved it to the utmost of their limited means. But economic education is a plant of slow growth . . . in a soil long productive of the rankest weeds.[13]

De Leon's judgment of the German-Americans of the International resembles Sorge's judgment of Weydemeyer. They did the best they could in a country that was not ready for them.

There is less charity in evidence in the appraisals of De Leon himself. In the opinion of Schlueter's *Volkszeitung* the existence of De Leon's Socialist Trade and Labor Alliance prevented a socialist victory over Gompers in the AFL. Philip S. Foner supports this contention with the argument that "the continuing rank-and-file pressure against bureaucracy and class collaboration was deprived of its actual and potential leaders precisely at the time when it was possible for socialists to supply such leadership." According to Selig Perlman, De Leon's tactics were the supreme disaster for socialism in the United States.[14] It would push the idea of American exceptionalism too far to deny that the AFL might have been won for socialist politics and that a great party of reform based on the labor movement might have emerged in the United States at the turn of the century. If De Leon had understood in the nineties (as he did in 1908) that American conditions justified a broad, multi-hued socialist party based on the unions, it seems likely that the split which rent the SLP in 1899 would have been avoided and that the socialist movement after 1900 would have been intellectually and numerically stronger than in fact it was. Such a movement might well have been under the sway of Berger and Hillquit for years or decades; but within it the influence of the Marxist left would have been proportionate to its influence in the Socialist party of Debs.

## The Socialist Party and the Tradition

The Socialist party was a coalition of three major tendencies. Its largely western left rallied around Debs and Haywood. Its center, largely eastern in strength, had the Kautskyan Morris Hillquit as its spokesman. Its right wing of municipal reformers based in Milwaukee, Reading, Schenectady, and other Socialist-run cities found a leader in Victor Berger.[15] Until about 1908 the three tendencies coexisted in the party under an administration which respected the principle of autonomy. As long as the national office of the party gave free rein, a wide span of labor and middle-class radicalisms jostled each other in the SP.

Though Debs was the popular leader of the party, the party was not his; and it was not Hillquit's or Berger's either. The views of these leaders were too stable and definite to allow any of them to be thought of as the representative man of the heterogeneous SP. A figure like Brownson would more nearly succeed in personifying the SP than would any of them. For one finds in Brownson the fierce indignation against exploitation, the faith in political action, and the personal independence of party machinery which animated Debs. One finds, too, the step-at-a-time reformism and the radicalism ravaged by hostility to the Negro cause which characterized Berger. One finds as well the easy familiarity with the last word in European social thought of a Hillquit. Finally, one finds the apocalyptic rhetoric of the Wobblies and the social gospel language of love of George D. Herron and Walter Rauschenbusch. The SP was full of traditional American radicalism. But one cannot discover the whole politics of the SP in the mind of Brownson. The stream of German-American Marxism, more through men of the Kautskyan center—like Hillquit and Schlueter—than through Berger, contributed significantly to the SP. There was also a De Leonist influence which made itself felt chiefly through Debs.

"By 1901," wrote Lillian Symes and Travers Clement,

> the majority of the active American socialists were reacting violently against the fratricidal struggles, the scholastic dissentions and the heresy hunts which had marked the past ten years of radical

history. The ghost of "De Leonism" so haunted the new organization through all its formative years that its members were ready to lean over backwards to prevent the rise of a new "pope," another *People*.[16]

This is true of members of the SP who had been in the SLP in the nineties and had broken with De Leon in 1899. No doubt it is true of many other SP members as well, but it is not true of Debs himself. The political fact was that former SLP members who joined the SP as a rule were pro-AFL as well as anti-De Leon. But Debs since 1893 had opposed craft and promoted industrial unionism. His American Railway Union was dual to the railroad craft organizations. Ex-SLP members like Hillquit and Schlueter were politically farther from De Leon than Debs was at the time the SP was formed. But just how close to the politics of the SLP did Debs come? Let us take the testimony of Debs and De Leon themselves on this point.

In 1905 at the founding convention of the IWW, Debs had this to say about his relations with De Leon:

> We have not been the best of friends in the past (laughter), but the whirligig of time brings about some wonderful changes. I find myself breaking away from some men I have been in very close touch with, and getting in close touch with some men from whom I have been widely separated.[17]

Debs, it is clear from this, was well aware that support for the IWW and collaboration with De Leon would involve strife with other leaders of the SP, in particular those with AFL connections. Nevertheless Debs persisted in his course, though not to the point of split with the center and right wings of the SP. Two essays contributed by Debs to the *International Socialist Review* in 1912 and 1914 show the continuing closeness of Debs's standpoint to De Leon's. In the first of these articles Debs was trying to ward off a split in the SP between the pro-IWW left and the pro-AFL center and right. He pleaded for an authentic American socialism which would devise tactics without respect to "the precedents of other countries. We have to develop our own and they must be adapted to the American people and to American conditions."

Debs knew, as De Leon realized in 1908, that there was no immediate prospect of consensus on tactics. "We are in for a lively time at the very best before we work out these differences and settle down to a policy of united and constructive work for Socialism instead of spending so much time and energy lampooning one another."

Like the De Leon who linked himself to Thomas Skidmore, Debs repudiated bourgeois property rights. "As a revolutionist I can have no respect for capitalist property laws, nor the least scruple about violating them. I hold such laws to have been enacted through chicanery, fraud and corruption, with the sole end of dispossessing, robbing, and enslaving the working class." Also, like De Leon, is Debs's dissociation from the Wobblies' verbal cult of violence:

> There have been times in the past, and there are countries today where the frenzied deed of a glorious fanatic like old John Brown seems to have been inspired by Jehovah himself, but I am now dealing with the twentieth century and with the United States.

Under American conditions, Debs continued, "a great body of organized workers, such as the Socialist movement, cannot predicate its tactical procedure upon such exceptional instances" as those which might justify resort to violence. As with De Leon, so with Debs the key to non-violent revolution was consciousness: "To the extent that the working class has power based on its class-consciousness, force is unnecessary; to the extent that power is lacking, force can only result in harm." To those IWW leaders who toyed with the idea of substituting force for mass support Debs spoke of the need to work "in the broad open light of day. Nothing can be done by stealth that can be of advantage in this country. . . . The American workers are law-abiding and no amount of sneering or derision will alter that fact." If the IWW "ignores political action, or treats it with contempt by advising the workers to 'strike at the ballot box with an ax,' they will regard it as an anarchist organization, and it will never be more than a small fraction of the labor movement."

Debs was more flexible than De Leon customarily was when

he urged "industrial independent organization, especially among the millions who have not yet been organized at all" while simultaneously advocating "the 'boring from within' for all that can be accomplished by industrial unionists in the craft unions." But he was just as unbending as De Leon in his attitude toward the AFL bureaucracy: "The Socialist Party cannot be neutral on the union question. . . . I am opposed under all circumstances to any party alliances or affiliations with reactionary trade unions." This attitude was connected with the De Leonist stress he placed on the importance of class consciousness: "The sound education of the workers and their thorough organization, both economic and political, on the basis of the class struggle, must precede their emancipation."[18]

In 1913 Debs wrote "A Plea for Solidarity" in which he urged reunification of the syndicalist majority and the De Leonist minority of the IWW on the basis of the De Leonist program which was "cornerstoned in the true principles of unionism in reference to political action." In the same article he sought to unify the SP and the SLP and expressed the conviction that unity of socialists on the industrial and political fields would produce in America "the foremost proletarian revolutionary movement in the world."[19]

In retrospection a few months before his death in 1914, De Leon gauged his closeness to Debs. He recalled that after the split of 1899 the anti-De Leon SLP members "fled for asylum to the political movement that Eugene V. Debs had just started in the west." Toward the Debs movement De Leon had been "hopefully expectant":

Debs was no A.F. of L. man. Far otherwise and to the contrary. He had no superstitious horror for "rival" or "dual" unions; nor did he entertain any superstitious reverence for "boring from within." If the structure of an economic organization was wrong and there was no other way to mend matters, he believed in setting up another union, and he boldly practiced what he preached. What is more, he rose to prominence as a leader of just such practices. Indeed, it was at the time, and even since then off and on, hard to tell Debs from the S.L.P. so far as the union question was concerned. The expectation seemed justified that the political movement which Debs conjured into existence as a leader in the formation of revolutionary unions, would be animated by his breath. As a consequence, it was expected that the seceders from the S.L.P. would be captured by the political asylum to which they fled. As a further consequence, it was hoped and even expected in 1900, and the expectation rearose in 1905 when the I.W.W. was launched with the joint assistance of Debs and the S.L.P., that A.F. of L.ism would be uprooted. It all happened the other way. The seceders from the S.L.P. captured their political asylum; the A.F. of L. was "saved."[20]

It was a paradox to which Debs himself bowed that he, the most attractive and persuasive of leaders, was not a maker of policy for the SP. Debs elected to carry on an energetic propaganda before the broadest public he could reach but declined to take part in the factional in-fighting of the SP. This side of his political behavior must be contrasted to De Leon's. Perhaps Debs's reputation for benevolence depended on his refusal to fight with the determination of a De Leon to persuade the SP to adopt his tactics. Debs had justified factional ruthlessness at the IWW's founding convention. "A man," he had said, "is not worthy, in my judgment, to enlist in the services of the working class unless he has the moral stamina, if need be, to break asunder all personal relations to serve that class."[21] But Debs did not subsequently perform according to the code which he then sanctioned. There was in Debs a rare combination of fiery militancy and fraternity; he synthesized a near-De Leonist Marxism with the practice of brotherhood:

> We need above all the real Socialist spirit, which expresses itself in boundless enthusiasm, energetic action, and the courage to dare and do all things in the service of the cause. We need to *be* comrades in all the term implies and to help and cheer and strengthen one another in the daily struggle. If the "love of comrades" is but a barren ideality in the Socialist movement, then there is no place for it in the heart of mankind."[22]

The fraternal Debs has passed into legend. It would be well if the legend could incorporate the fact that the fraternal Debs was also the revolutionary man of action who went to the country with the De Leonist version of Marxism and evoked a greater response than has yet come to another American labor radical. It must be that he was important for his ideas as well as for himself.

### The Communist Party and the Tradition

The Socialist party harbored Americanizers of Marx as well as reformists who were intent on adapting their socialism to middle-class sensibilities. The Communist party after a few years of factional turbulence was a monolithic structure inhibiting diversity of tactical opinion within its ranks. Monolithism discouraged the growth of distinctively American revolutionary and gradualist tendencies within the CP. But even if the party had maintained a more liberal internal regime the party would still have been spellbound by the Russian Revolution. The awesome authority of Bolshevism among the American Communists was by itself probably enough to prevent an American version of Marxism from developing within it. Furthermore, the Russians did not rely on spells. Palpable strings were pulled from Moscow to promote, demote, and otherwise animate American CP leaders. The party's politics were not primarily an interaction between Marxism and the American environment. The Comintern reduced Marxism in the United States to a colonial phenomenon. The SLP in the eighteen-eighties had voluntarily aped the German Social Democracy until De Leon transformed it into an independent American party. For a generation the CP imitated the Russian mother party, and in this case the aping was both voluntary and by command.[23] The result was an organization whose tactical ideas could not for long be taken seriously. To the extent that it was at war with the American social order the CP tended toward exoticism; to the extent that it adapted itself to the American environment it tended to obliterate itself. The feat of being American and radical at the same time seemed beyond its strength. That inability was shared by leading Communists whose expulsion from the party freed them to experiment with Americanizing Marx. Bertram D. Wolfe and Earl Browder are cases in point. Wolfe and Browder each wrote essays entitled *Marx and America*. Wolfe was a leader of the Jay Lovestone faction of the American CP in the twenties. He was expelled in 1929 during the international purge of right wing Communists associated with Nikolai Bukharin. Browder, the principal American beneficiary of that purge, led the CP as its general secretary from 1930 to 1945. The *Marx and America* by Wolfe appeared in 1934, the one by Browder in 1959. They provide an idea of what has passed for Americanization of Marx among the founders of the CP.

The thesis of Wolfe's work is that while Marx understood America, his followers have not. The German-Americans are whipping-boys Wolfe uses as stand-ins for the Browder-led CP. "Why," he asks,

> did the American "Marxists" of German origin fail to influence the young American working class just beginning to feel its power and to organize on a national scale in the last quarter of the 19th century? Primarily because they failed utterly to make a realistic analysis of American conditions, of the specific national characteristics or peculiarities of the country in which they sought to give their correct general theory concrete application.

This charge is unsupported with specific counts. He mentions Sorge only as the recipient of letters from Marx and Engels. His discussion of Marxist thought in America excludes all mention of De Leon and Debs. He freely generalizes that "except for fragmentary hints from the pens of Marx, Engels and Lenin, and partial beginnings made recently by American Marxians, the development of 'American Marxism' (in the sense of the application of Marxian theory to the analysis of American conditions) has scarcely begun."[24] What lends significance to Wolfe's slight book is that next to De Leon's protégé Louis C. Fraina, Wolfe was the most enterprising scholar in the early Communist movement. The American past of the movement was a blank slate to him. The task of the Lovestone group was to work out an American Marxism *de novo* with reference to the texts of Marx, Engels, and Lenin but without reference to the thought and experience of earlier Marxists in America. Like the fundamentalism of the Protestant Reformation, Wolfe's American Marxism was to apprehend truth directly from the inspired word. It would see in the tradition of American Marxism only an exasperating barrier separating the seekers from the prophets of old.

This attitude toward the German Americans and toward De Leon and Debs shows the Lovestone group to have been as Russified as were their rivals of the official Communist party. While Wolfe was promising to piece out the ideas of Marx and Engels on America, "fragments of a gigantic structure," he and other Lovestoneites were busy defending Stalinism in Russia, including the first two great Moscow purge trials. They balked at accepting the trial and execution of their Russian mentor Bukharin in 1938, for with Bukharin perished the last hope of their reconciliation with Stalin and the official CP. Within a year they relinquished their pretensions to being the architects of an American Marxism; they dissolved their group in 1939.[25] For the Lovestoneites as later for Browder, the shattering of the image of Russia as the holy land of revolution apparently left them without a reason for being radical. There could be no more compelling evidence of the exotic nature of their Marxism.

American Communism's days of strength occurred while Browder led the party. The CP entered the depression with seven thousand members. By 1938 the membership had risen to eighty thousand and it had decisive influence in a third of the new industrial unions of the CIO. Though its prestige among intellectuals was severely damaged when it defended the Stalin-Hitler Pact of 1939, the party maintained its strength in the labor movement until the onset of the cold war. Its support dribbled away in the late forties and early fifties. It received mortal wounds in 1956 from Krushchev's denunciation of the crimes of Stalin and from the Soviet suppression of the Hungarian revolution. The American CP entered the sixties with fewer members than it had in 1930.[26]

The purging of Browder in 1945 coincided with the beginning of the party's eclipse. That coincidence gives rise to the suspicion that a Browderite version of Marxism had possibilities in America which were nipped in the bud. There seems little substance behind that suspicion since the CP under Browder never tried to throw off its dependence on the moral authority of the Russians. Yet there was something about the CP of the Browder period linking it to earlier American labor radicalism. The CP developed a self-defeating *Realpolitik* reminiscent of the tactics which had marked and undercut the radical career of Brownson before the Civil War. In the last phase of Browder's leadership, the years between the Nazi invasion of Russia in 1941 and the close of the war, the CP pursued Brownsonian tactics. As Brownson had once turned his back on the social radicalism of his generation for the sake of the Jacksonian coalition, so the CP under Browder told the Negroes to forego the struggle for equality, and unionists to refrain from strikes for the sake of the war and for the sake of perpetuating the war-time coalition between the United States and Russia. This policy reduced the radicalism of the CP to a matter of tradition and sentiment. Such a radicalism depended on emotional ties with the Soviet Union. What might happen to it when a Communist severed his ties with Russia can be seen in Browder's *Marx and America*.

Unlike Wolfe's essay, Browder's is not a fundamentalist tract. Like Wolfe's essay, Browder's is the work of a man unfamiliar with the pre-CP history of American labor radicalism. A sense of performing pioneer intellectual labor consequently pervades both essays.

Browder's awareness of American labor history is disclosed in several passages of *Marx and America*. Once Browder scolds Hermann Schlueter for having "perpetuated the dogmatic position that wage labor is merely a disguised version of chattel slavery." Poor Schlueter was only sympathizing with a statement of William Sylvis that "a slavery exists in our land worse than ever existed under the old slave system." But for Browder, Schlueter's use of this quotation shows "how the early Socialist movement in America divorced itself from the mainstream of the national working-class development and from the nation's history through dogmatism."[27] Sylvis, the foremost workers' leader of the eighteen-sixties, is represented as himself out of touch with the workers

189

because he despised conditions in the factories of the Gilded Age. At another point Browder observes that "the insistence of early American socialists upon a dogmatic subsistence-wage theory (or even upon an 'iron law' in the case of De Leon and the Lassalleans) drove the American labor movement away from Marxism and all theory."[28] This remark could not have been made by a writer acquainted with De Leon's discussion of the relation between human needs and workingclass misery.

Mention of the "iron law" brings us to the theme of Browder's book. Browder argues that Marx had two contradictory theories of wages and two contradictory images of the United States. One of Marx's theories was the Lassallean "iron law" that wages must hover at the subsistence minimum in a capitalist economy; the other was that wages include a culturally determined element which may, as it has in America, bring the standard of wages considerably above the subsistence level. Marx mistook the prevalent reason for high wages in the United States. He supposed they resulted from the country's colonial and agrarian economy and that capitalist industrial development would destroy the high wage standard, reducing the American workers to the subsistence level. Browder sets out to correct Marx by showing that high wages have made American capitalism strong. They have stimulated technology and expanded production and accumulation. Since the beginning of America the workers and the employers have been spiralling together to affluence. Marx and his American followers never understood this because their "old theory of the subsistence wage emphasized the basic confrontation of employer versus worker, of labor versus capital." Browder presents his thoughts as a contribution to Marxian theory which "closes the abyss that for so long separated Marxism from the American labor movement and from American experience in general."[29] But if his emendation of Marxism is still Marxism, then all labor leaders who decry the class struggle and affirm the common interest of labor and capital are Marxist without knowing it. Browder's book does provide a solution to the problems of Marxism in the United States; it is not, however, the solution of an Americanizer of Marx. The historic aim of the Americanizers has not been to make

Marxism palatable to the liberal-reformist union officialdom, but to radicalize the labor movement.

Through Browder's *Marx and America* runs an implicit identification of the level of wages and the level of well-being of the workers. The Marxist concept of alienation is not once alluded to in this work purportedly concerned with the relevance of Marx to American experience. Browder does not view the condition of the working class as a complex of psychological, physiological, and economic phenomena; he considers it only from the wage standpoint. Perhaps that is why Browder shows no trace of the moral fire with which Marx responded to the condition of the workers when he wrote in *Capital* that:

> All means for the development of production . . . mutilate the laborer into a fragment of a man, degrade him to the level of an appendage of a machine, destroy every remnant of charm in his work and turn it into hated toil; they estrange him from the intellectual possibilities of the labour-process in the same proportion as science is incorporated in it as an independent power. . . . As capital accumulates, the lot of the labourer, be his payment high or low, must grow worse. . . . Accumulation of wealth at one pole is, therefore, at the same time accumulation of misery, agony, of toil, slavery, ignorance, brutality, mental degradation, at the opposite pole.[30]

Browder, in contrast to Marx, is not aroused by the revolutionary aim of restoring human dignity to the work process. For Browder the main American problem is to stimulate production under the present social order without regard to most of the aspects of workingclass life which worried Marx. Discarding the revolutionary Marxist goal of social ownership of the productive wealth, Browder cautions that "governmental intervention in the productive process . . . should be the last resort. . . . Removal of obstacles to progress need not be wholesale overturns, but may be discriminating remedies for precisely defined difficulties."[31] It would appear that the only thing which survives out of Browder's Communist past is the bureaucratic prose of the general secretary. But even while Browder was recommending all deliberate speed in social evolution a new generation of Americans was getting ready to demand "Freedom Now" and to explain "Why We Can't Wait." The Negro upsurge, however, has not yet had a leavening effect on the labor movement. Will it ever?

Every American generation since the eighteen-twenties has witnessed a significant expression of labor radicalism. It seems likely that there will be new expressions of it and that labor radicalism will be one of the forms of revolt to attract the generation now of college age. The great uncertainty would seem to lie in whether the next labor radicalism will be more conscious and more powerful than its predecessors. When the future dispells this uncertainty one of two historical estimates of the modern working class will have been vindicated: Thomas Jefferson's or Karl Marx's. Jefferson thought that the class of wage workers created by capitalism would prove politically and morally impotent, but Marx had faith that the victims of modern society would learn to free themselves. The scales of prophecy are still balanced. Experience has battered the conscience and depressed the self-confidence of the labor movement; but in the waves of reform turbulence which occasionally sweep the United States the role of labor has grown. Unless this pattern has finally fulfilled itself, the story of the Americanizers of Marx is not yet at an end.

# notes

**Chapter 1**

1. Hegel, *Vorlesungen die Philosophie der Geschichte, Saemtliche Werke,* ed. Hermann Glockner (Stuttgart, 1928), XI, 123, 129. Passages from works in German by Hegel, Herman Schlueter, and Friedrich Sorge are translated by the current author.
2. Quoted by Philo Ramm, *Ferdinand Lassalle als Rechts-und-Sozialphilosoph* (Vienna, 1953), p. 34.
3. *The Eighteenth Brumaire of Louis Bonaparte, Selected Works,* ed. V. Adoratsky (New York, 1935), II, 324.
4. For Turner's view, see *The Frontier in American History* (New York, 1920), pp. 1–36; see also Henry Nash Smith, *Virgin Land: The American West as Symbol and Myth* (Cambridge, Mass., 1950), pp. 250–60.
5. Henry Christman, *Tin Horns and Calico: A Decisive Episode in the Emergence of Democracy* (New York, 1945), p. 20.
6. New York *Times,* March 14, 1961, p. 12.
7. *Warum gibt es in den Vereinigten Staaten Keinen Sozialismus* (Tuebingen, 1906).
8. *Rich Lands and Poor: The Road to World Prosperity* (New York, 1958).
9. Marx, *Selected Writings in Sociology and Social Philosophy,* ed. T. B. Bottomore and Maximilian Rubel (London, 1956), p. 232.
10. *The Complete Works of Ralph Waldo Emerson,* ed. Edward Waldo Emerson (Boston, 1903–1904), III, 58.
11. *Selected Writings in Sociology,* pp. 68–69.
12. Emerson, *Works,* I, 395.
13. Ibid., pp. 452, 453–54.
14. *The Writings of Henry David Thoreau,* ed. Bradford Torrey and F. H. Allen (Boston, 1906), II, 59–60, 102–3, 130–31.
15. Marx, *Selected Works,* I, 208, 215, 218, 226.
16. Ibid., 207–8.
17. Cf. Marx, *Selected Works,* I, 210.
18. Ibid., 208–9.
19. Emerson, *Works,* I, 383–84.
20. Marx, *Selected Works,* I, 238–39.
21. Emerson, III, 254, 266–67.
22. *Selected Works,* I, 228.
23. Emerson, I, 365–66, 368.
24. *Selected Works,* II, 324.
25. Ibid., I, 210.
26. Emerson, I, 369–70.
27. *Selected Writings in Sociology,* pp. 245–46.

28. Emerson, I, 453, 454.
29. Herman Melville, *Battle Pieces and Aspects of the War* (New York, 1866), pp. 86–87.
30. John R. Commons et al., *History of Labour in the United States* (New York, 1918, 1934), I, 413–15; Philip S. Foner, *History of the Labor Movement in the United States* (New York, 1947), I, 226; Carl Wittke, *The Irish in America* (Baton Rouge, 1956), pp. 23–24, 31, 42, 216–22.
31. Carl Wittke, *Refugees of Revolution: The German Forty-Eighters in America* (Philadelphia, 1952), p. 43.
32. Friedrich A. Sorge, "Die Arbeiterbewegung in den Vereinigten Staaten," *Neue Zeit*, XI (1890), 198; Wittke, *The Irish*, p. 221; Commons, II, 181–91, 276.
33. Hans Gerth (ed.), *The First International: Minutes of the Hague Congress of 1872* (Madison, 1958), p. 197.
34. Carl Wittke, *The German Language Press in America* (Lexington, 1957), pp. 103–63.
35. *Selected Works*, II, 23.
36. Carl Wittke, *The Utopian Communist: A Biography of Wilhelm Weitling* (Baton Rouge, 1950), p. 213.

Chapter 2
1. Thoreau, *Writings*, II, 8.
2. Commons, *History of Labour*, I, 169.
3. Brownson, *The Works of Orestes A. Brownson*, ed. Henry F. Brownson (Detroit, 1885–87), V, 62.
4. Commons, I, 232.
5. Brownson, *Works*, V, 63.
6. Isaac T. Hecker, "Dr. Brownson and the Workingman's Party of Fifty Years Ago," *Catholic World*, XIV (May 1887), 201–3.
7. Brownson, *Works*, V, 63.
8. Hecker, pp. 204–5.
9. Henry F. Brownson, *Orestes A. Brownson's Early Life* (Detroit, 1898), p. 118.
10. "Grund's Americans," *Boston Quarterly Review*, I (1838), 191 (cited hereafter as *BQR*). For the ten-hour-day movement, see Commons, I, 234–35, 284–395.
11. "The Laboring Classes," Pt. 1, *BQR*, III (1840), 365.
12. Thoreau, *Writings*, II, 13.
13. "Democracy and Christianity," *BQR*, I (1838), 471.
14. "Tendency of Modern Civilization," *BQR*, I (1838), 237–38.
15. "Conversations with a Radical," *BQR*, IV (1841), 26.
16. "Specimens of Foreign Literature," *BQR*, I (1838), 440–41.
17. "Introductory Statement," *BQR*, III (1840), 17.
18. "The Laboring Classes," Pt. 2, *BQR*, III (1840), 477–80, 502; "Introductory Statement," *BQR*, III, 18; "The Laboring Classes," Pt. 2, *BQR*, III, 484, 492–95; "The Rights of Women," *BQR*, II (1839), 350–78.
19. "The Laboring Classes," Pt. 1, *BQR*, III, 391; "Our Future Policy," *BQR*, IV (1841), 82.
20. "A Discourse on Lying," *BQR*, III (1840), 413.

21. "The Laboring Classes," Pt. 2, *BQR*, III, 474.
22. Ibid., Pt. 1, pp. 366, 367.
23. Ibid., Pt. 2, pp. 472–74.
24. "Address to the Workingmen," *BQR*, IV (1841), 114.
25. "The Laboring Classes," Pt. 2, *BQR*, III, 506.
26. Ibid., Pt. 1, p. 393.
27. "Literary Notes," *BQR*, IV (1841), 391.
28. "Democracy and Reform," *BQR*, II (1839), 478–517.
29. "Slavery-Abolitionism," *BQR*, I (1838), 240.
30. "Abolition Proceedings," *BQR*, I (1838), 496–97.
31. Ibid.
32. Brownson, *Works*, XVII, 196.
33. Ibid., XV, 83.
34. "The Laboring Classes," Pt. 2, *BQR*, III, 471.
35. *Karl Marx and Frederick Engels on Britain* (Moscow, 1955), p. 149.
36. "The Laboring Classes," Pt. 2, *BQR*, III, 468.
37. Quoted in Lillian Symes and Travers Clement, *Rebel America: The Story of Social Revolt in the United States* (New York, 1934), pp. 87–88.
38. "The Laboring Classes," Pt. 2, *BQR*, III, 467.
39. "Our Future Policy," *BQR*, IV (1841), 85, 90.
40. Brownson, *Works*, XV, 259.
41. "Our Future Policy," *BQR*, IV, 70.
42. Ibid., p. 90.
43. Brownson, *Works*, V, 121.
44. Arthur M. Schlesinger, Jr., *Orestes A. Brownson: A Pilgrim's Progress* (Boston, 1939), pp. 244–50.
45. Brownson, *Works*, XVIII, 191.
46. Marx and Engels, *The Civil War in the United States* (New York, 1937), p. 82.
47. Marx, *Capital: A Critique of Political Economy* (Chicago, 1912), I, 329.
48. C. Vann Woodward, *Reunion and Reaction: The Compromise of 1877 and the End of Reconstruction* (Boston, 1951), pp. 4, 246.
49. *Capital*, p. 329.
50. Brownson, *Works*, XVII, 546, 548.
51. Ibid., XVIII, 191–92.
52. Ibid., XVI, 7.
53. The account of Kriege is compiled from Herman Schlueter, *Die Anfaenge der deutschen Arbeiterbewegung in Amerika* (Stuttgart, 1907), pp. 29–37, 189–90; William F. Kamman, *Socialism in German-American Literature* (Philadelphia, 1917), p. 19; Wittke, *The Utopian Communist*, pp. 118–20.
54. Hawthorne, *American Notebooks*, June 1, 1841.

Chapter 3

1. Sources for the sketch of Weydemeyer's life are Karl Obermann, *Joseph Weydemeyer: Pioneer of American Socialism* (New York, 1947), pp. 7–35; Schlueter, *Die Anfaenge*, pp. 157–59.
2. Obermann, pp. 28, 29.

3. Marx and Engels, *Letters to Americans: 1848–1895*, ed. Alexander Trachtenberg (New York, 1953), p. 26.
4. Sources for the sketch of Sorge's early life are Herman Schlueter, *Die Internationale in Amerika: Ein Beitrag zur Geschichte der Arbeiterbewegung in den Vereinigten Staaten* (Chicago, 1918), pp. 411–13; Sorge, "Erinerungen eines Achtundviersigers," *Neue Zeit*, XVII, Pt. 2 (1899), 150–448 passim.
5. Gustav Mayer, *Friedrich Engels: A Biography* (New York, 1936), pp. 116–18; Schlueter, *Die Internationale*, p. 413.
6. "Friedrich Albert Sorge," *Neue Zeit*, XXV (1906), 145–47.
7. Obermann, p. 38; quoted from Paul Kampfmeyer, *Die Gesellschaft Internationale Revue fuer Sozialismus and Politik*, V (November 1928), 452–62.
8. Obermann, p. 40; *Neue Zeit*, XXV (1906), 101.
9. Obermann, p. 47; *Turn-Zeitung*, I (February 1852).
10. Ibid., p. 47; *Turn-Zeitung*, I (March 1852).
11. Obermann, p. 53.
12. Schlueter, *Die Anfaenge*, pp. 140–41.
13. Ibid., pp. 142–44.
14. Obermann, pp. 85–87.
15. Wittke, *The Utopian Communist*, pp. 118, 286; Schlueter, *Die Anfaenge*, p. 190; Commons, *History of Labour*, II, 10–11; Herman Schlueter, *Lincoln, Labor and Slavery* (New York, 1913), p. 73.
16. Obermann, pp. 83–84, 108.
17. Wittke, *The Utopian Communist*, pp. 119–20; Schlueter, *Die Anfaenge*, pp. 189–90; Kamman, *Socialism in German-American Literature*, p. 19.
18. See David Mitrany, *Marx Against the Peasant: A Study of Social Dogmatism* (Chapel Hill, 1951).
19. Kamman, p. 24; Wittke, *The German Language Press*, p. 92; Obermann, pp. 104–12.
20. Obermann, pp. 119–28; Friedrich A. Sorge, "Joseph Weydemeyer," *Pioneer Illustrirter Volks-Kalender* (New York, 1897), p. 60; Kamman, p. 24.
21. Obermann, pp. 131–40.
22. Wittke, *The Utopian Communist*, p. 211.
23. "Friedrich Albert Sorge" (obituary), *Neue Zeit*, XVI (1907), 488; Marx and Engels, *Briefwechsel* (Berlin, 1950), IV, 620.
24. Schlueter, *Die Internationale*, pp. 412–14; on Heinzen and Marxism, see Carl Wittke, *Against the Current: The Life of Karl Heinzen* (Chicago, 1945).
25. Schlueter, *Die Anfaenge*, p. 161; Obermann, p. 92.
26. Schlueter, *Die Anfaenge*, p. 162; Obermann, pp. 92–93.
27. Schlueter, *Die Anfaenge*, p. 194, 197; Wittke, *The German Language Press*, p. 172.
28. Sorge, "Die Arbeiterbewegung in den Vereinigten Staaten," *Neue Zeit*, IX (1890), 194, 196.
29. Schlueter, *Die Anfaenge*, p. 198.
30. Schlueter, *Die Internationale*, p. 416.
31. Ibid., p. 417.
32. Marx, "Address and Provisional Rules of the Working Men's International Association," *Selected Works*, II, 432–35.
33. Commons, III, 205.

34. Marx, *Selected Works*, II, 440–41.
35. Ibid., I, 240.
36. G. M. Stekloff, *History of the First International* (London, 1928), pp. 76–78, 124–27, 249, 268.
37. Commons, III, 87; II, 63.
38. Marx, *Value, Price and Profit*, ed. Eleanor Marx Aveling (Chicago, n.d.), pp. 126–27.
39. Commons, II, 205–7.
40. Ibid., III, 87, 152–53.
41. Schlueter, *Die Internationale*, p. 118.
42. Commons, III, 153–54; Schlueter, *Die Internationale*, p. 173; Morris Hillquit, *History of Socialism in the United States* (5th ed.; New York, 1910), pp. 173–74.
43. Commons, II, 152.
44. Schlueter, *Die Internationale*, p. 67.
45. John R. Commons, "Labor Movement," *Encyclopedia of the Social Sciences*, VIII (1932).
46. Marx, *Selected Works*, I, 240, 252–53; Commons, *History of Labour*, III, 218–19; Selig Perlman, *A Theory of the Labor Movement* (New York, 1928), pp. 201–303.
47. Friedrich A. Sorge, *Socialism and the Worker* (New York, 1876), p. 14.
48. Sorge, "Die Arbeiterbewegung," *Neue Zeit*, X (1891–92), p. 393.
49. Schlueter, *Die Internationale*, pp. 115–22; Kamman, p. 27; Wittke, *The German Language Press*, p. 165; Commons, *History of Labor*, III, 225.

Chapter 4

1. Marx, *Selected Works*, II, 624.
2. Schlueter, *Die Internationale*, p. 136; Oscar Sherwin, *Prophet of Liberty: The Life and Times of Wendell Phillips* (New York, 1958), p. 599.
3. Commons, *History of Labour*, III, 210.
4. Sorge, "Die Arbeiterbewegung," *Neue Zeit*, X (1891–92), 392.
5. Quoted in C. Vann Woodward, *Tom Watson: Agrarian Rebel* (New York, 1938), p. 406.
6. Sorge, "Die Arbeiterbewegung," p. 392.
7. Marx, *Selected Works*, II, 581.
8. Sorge, "Die Arbeiterbewegung," p. 393.
9. Ibid., p. 392.
10. Emanie Sachs, *The Terrible Siren, Victoria Woodhull* (New York, 1928), pp. 78–80, 118–19, 215.
11. Ibid., pp. 1–46.
12. Ibid., p. 80.
13. *Woodhull and Claflin's Weekly*, January 22, 1872.
14. Sachs, p. 147.
15. Ibid., pp. 218–19.
16. *Woodhull and Claflin's Weekly*, December 28, 1872.
17. Sachs, pp. 288–91.
18. *The Scarlet Letter* (New York, 1947), p. 25.

19. John R. Commons et al., *A Documentary History of American Industrial Society* (Cleveland, 1910–11), IX, 360.
20. Schlueter, *Die Internationale*, p. 150.
21. Commons, *Documentary History*, IX, 360.
22. Schlueter, *Die Internationale*, p. 154; *Woodhull and Claflin's Weekly*, March 2, 1872; Commons, *History of Labour*, II, 210.
23. Schlueter, *Die Internationale*, pp. 155–57, 161; Commons, *History of Labour*, II, 212.
24. Schlueter, *Die Internationale*, p. 155.
25. *Woodhull and Claflin's Weekly*, December 3, 1871; March 2, 1872.
26. Marx and Engels, *Letters to Americans*, pp. 89–90.
27. Commons, *Documentary History*, IX, 361–64; Schlueter, *Die Internationale*, p. 150.
28. Gerth, *The First International*, pp. 196–98, 213.
29. *Woodhull and Claflin's Weekly*, March 22, 1873.
30. *Moby Dick, or the Whale*, ed. Luther S. Mansfield and Howard P. Vincent (New York, 1952), pp. 166–67.
31. Gerth, p. 242.
32. Commons, *History of Labour*, III, 218.
33. Ibid., III, 219–22.
34. Schlueter, *Die Internationale*, p. 332.
35. Stekloff, *History of the First International*, pp. 285–86.
36. Ibid., p. 425 n.
37. Schlueter, *Die Internationale*, pp. 378–79, 399.
38. Commons, *History of Labour*, III, 276, 286.
39. Ibid., III, 306; Schlueter, *Die Internationale*, p. 420.
40. Howard Quint, *The Forging of American Socialism: Origins of the Modern Movement* (Columbia, 1953), pp. 33–42.

Chapter 5
1. Marx, *Selected Works*, I, 240.
2. W. J. Ghent, "Daniel De Leon," *DAB*, V (1930); Olive M. Johnson, "Daniel De Leon—Our Comrade," *Daniel De Leon: The Man and His Work*, ed. Henry Kuhn (4th ed.; New York, 1934), pp. 88–90; Arnold Petersen, *Daniel De Leon: Social Architect* (New York, 1941), I, 113; M. Beer, *Fifty Years of International Socialism* (New York, 1935), p. 110.
3. Kuhn, p. 120.
4. James B. Stalvey, "Daniel De Leon: A Study of Marxian Orthodoxy in the United States" (unpublished Ph.D. dissertation, University of Illinois, 1947), p. 27.
5. Petersen, p. 14.
6. New York *Herald Tribune*, July 29, 1894; Stalvey, p. 24.
7. Kuhn, pp. 90–91.
8. New York *Tribune*, October 2, 1886.
9. Stalvey, p. 39; Joseph Dorfman, "The Seligman Correspondence, III," *Political Science Quarterly*, LVI (1941), 398.
10. Lester Luntz, "Daniel De Leon and the Movement for Social Reform, 1886–

1896," (unpublished M.A. thesis, Columbia University, 1939), p. 11; New York *Tribune*, October 24, 1887; New York *Standard*, November 5, 1887.
11. Marx, *Selected Works*, I, 227.
12. Marx and Engels, *Letters to Americans*, p. 288.
13. Dorfman, p. 398; Stalvey, p. 39.
14. Petersen, p. 16 n.; *Daily People*, October 9, 1904; Henry David, *The Haymarket Affair* (New York, 1936), p. 412.
15. Luntz, pp. 23–26, 29; *The People*, August 2, 1891; Kuhn, p. 4.
16. Stalvey, p. 41.
17. Joseph Schlossberg, *The Workers and Their World: Aspects of the Workers' Struggle at Home and Abroad* (New York, 1935), p. 87.
18. George Simpson, "The American Karl Marx," *American Mercury*, XXXIII (1934), 65.
19. Stalvey, p. 27.
20. *The People*, June 26, 1898.
21. Kuhn, p. 42; Bertha De Leon, "The Nineties with De Leon," *Fifty Years of American Marxism* (New York, 1941), p. 23.
22. *The People*, April 1891; June 7, 1891; September 25, 1892; August 13, 1893; May 30, 1894.
23. De Leon, "Reform or Revolution," *Socialist Landmarks: Four Addresses* (New York, 1952), p. 57.
24. [Henry Demarest Lloyd], "The Progressive Movement Abroad," *Progressive Review* (London), I (1897), 361; Quint, *The Forging of American Socialism*, pp. 244–45.
25. Laurence Gronlund, *The Co-operative Commonwealth* (Boston, 1884), p. 9; Quint, p. 28.
26. Ira Kipnis, *The American Socialist Movement: 1897–1912* (New York, 1952), p. 422; Lewis Coser and Irving Howe, *The American Communist Party: A Critical History (1919–1957)* (Boston, 1957), pp. 385–86.
27. Commons, *History of Labour*, II, 196–202, 483.
28. Ibid., pp. 494–95, 519.
29. Kipnis, p. 15.
30. Commons, *History of Labour*, II, 509–14.
31. Kuhn, pp. 14, 19.
32. Bert Cochran, *American Labor in Midpassage* (New York, 1959), pp. 16–17.
33. Foner, *History of the Labor Movement*, II, 258.
34. Marx, *Selected Works*, II, 215.
35. Paul F. Brissenden, *The I.W.W.: A Study of American Syndicalism* (New York, 1920), p. 83.
36. Kuhn, p. 8.
37. Ibid., p. 33; *Proceedings of the Ninth Annual Convention of the Socialist Labor Party (1896)* (New York, 1897), p. 30.
38. Foner, II, 298; Kipnis, p. 27.
39. *The People*, August 14, 1898.
40. SLP *Proc.*, *Ninth*, p. 29.
41. Herman Schlueter, *The Brewing Industry and the Brewery Workers' Movement in America* (Cincinnati, 1910), pp. 226–28; Kipnis, p. 195.

42. David J. Saposs, *Left Wing Unionism: A Study of Radical Policies and Tactics* (New York, 1926), passim.
43. Hillquit, *History of Socialism*, pp. 277–78.
44. *Proceedings of the First Convention of the Industrial Workers of the World* (New York, 1906), p. 151.
45. *The People*, November 27, 1898.
46. Howard Quint, "American Socialists and the Spanish-American War," *American Quarterly*, X (Summer 1958), 134–37.
47. *The People*, June 26, 1898.
48. Ibid., July 16, 1899.
49. Ibid., July 23, 1899.
50. Commons, *History of Labour*, II, 519–20.
51. *Proceedings of the Tenth Annual Convention of the Socialist Labor Party* (New York, 1901), pp. 293–94; *The People*, June 9, 1899.
52. David A. Shannon, *The Socialist Party of America* (New York, 1955), pp. 1–44.
53. *Volkszeitung*, April 25, 1899; quoted in Kuhn, *Daniel De Leon: The Man and His Work*, p. 125.
54. *The People*, May 1, 1899.
55. August Bebel, *Woman under Socialism*, trans. Daniel De Leon (New York, 1904), p. 372.
56. Marx and Engels, *The Russian Menace to Europe*, ed. Paul W. Blackstock (Glencoe, 1955), pp. 56–95.
57. *The People*, July 31, October 9, November 27, 1898.
58. G. D. H. Cole, *A History of Socialist Thought*, Vol. III: *The Second International: 1889–1914* (London and New York, 1958), pp. 12–13, 37.
59. In Daniel De Leon, *Flashlights of the Amsterdam Congress* (New York, 1929), pp. 148–49.
60. *Daily People*, January 17, March 14, 1901.
61. Kipnis, p. 118.
62. *Flashlights*, pp. 181–95.
63. Ibid., p. 193.
64. Ibid., pp. 164–71.
65. *IWW Proc.*, p. 147.
66. *A History of Trade Unionism in the United States* (New York, 1950), p. 177.
67. *Socialist Landmarks*, pp. 53–54.
68. *SLP Proc., Tenth*, p. 7.
69. Quoted in Petersen, *Daniel De Leon: Social Architect*, I, 92.
70. Kipnis, pp. 236–40.
71. *Two Pages from Roman History*, pp. 7–8, 46–60.
72. Ibid., pp. 71–80.
73. Ibid., pp. 82–88.
74. Ibid., p. 53.
75. *Socialist Landmarks*, p. 153.
76. *Daily People*, June 27, 1905.
77. *Socialist Landmarks*, pp. 177–90.
78. Ibid., pp. 197, 199, 228, 203.

79. Ibid., pp. 218. 221,
80. Ibid., pp. 224–25.
81. Brissenden, *The I.W.W.*, pp. 136–47, 220–26.
82. Ibid., p. 92.
83. *As to Politics* (3rd ed.; New York, 1921), pp. 6, 14–15.
84. Ibid., pp. 7, 64–65, 72.
85. Ibid, pp. 10, 17.
86. Ibid., p. 61.
87. Ibid., pp. 69, 78–79, 88.
88. Ibid., pp. 76, 89–90.
89. Ibid., pp. 107–8.
90. Ibid., pp. 109–10.
91. William D. Haywood, *Bill Haywood's Book* (New York, 1929), p. 221.
92. Marx, *Selected Works*, I, 240.
93. *Unity: An Address Delivered by Daniel De Leon at New Pythagoras Hall, New York, February 21, 1908* (New York, 1908), pp. 9–13, 15, 17, 19.
94. Kipnis, p. 207.
95. Kuhn, pp. 66–67.
96. *Unity*, pp. 3–4.
97. *SLP Proc., Tenth*, p. 97.
98. *The Ballot and the Class Struggle* (New York, 1935), pp. 12, 29.
99. *Abolition of Poverty* (New York, 1945), pp. 14–15.
100. Kipnis, pp. 133–34.
101. Marx and Engels, *Civil War in the United States*, p. 261.
102. *The People*, February 9, 1896.
103. *Ballot and the Class Struggle*, pp. 20, 48.
104. *Flashlights*, pp. 160, 218.
105. Translator's "Preface," *Woman under Socialism*, p. iii.
106. *Ballot and the Class Struggle*, pp. 12, 38–39, 43.
107. *Revolutionary Socialism in the U.S. Congress* (New York, 1931), p. 39.
108. *Ballot and the Class Struggle*, pp. 38, 48.
109. *The Life and Selected Writings of Thomas Jefferson*, ed. Adrienne Koch and William Peden (New York, 1944), p. 277.
110. *Russia in Revolution: Selected Editorials* (2nd ed.; New York, 1930), p. 11.

Chapter 6
1. *SLP Proc., Tenth*, pp. 86, 253.
2. Commons, *History of Labour*, I, 236–45.
3. "Our Future Policy," *BQR*, IV (1841), 82.
4. *Ballot and the Class Struggle*, pp. 6, 15.
5. Bebel, *Woman under Socialism*, pp. 320, 336.
6. The Laboring Classes," Pt. 2, *BQR*, III (1840), 508.
7. De Leon, *Russia in Revolution*, p. 19; *Daily People*, January 29, 1905.
8. De Leon, *Abolition of Poverty*, pp. 29–30.
9. *Daily People*, September 9, 1912; June 5, 1910.
10. Isaac T. Hecker, "Doctor Brownson and Bishop Fitzpatrick," *Catholic World*, XLV (April 1887), 6–7.
11. *Neue Zeit*, IX, Pt. 1 (1890), 201.

12. Schlueter, *Die Internationale,* pp. 119, 173, 399.
13. *The People,* May 1, 1899.
14. *Volkszeitung,* May 13, 1914; quoted in Kuhn, *Daniel De Leon: The Man and His Work,* p. 25; Foner, *History of the Labor Movement,* II, pp. 298–99.
15. Shannon, *The Socialist Party of America,* pp. 12–42; Kipnis, *The American Socialist Movement,* pp. 107–8.
16. Symes and Clement, *Rebel America,* p. 219.
17. *IWW Proc.,* p. 145.
18. "Sound Socialist Tactics," *Writings and Speeches of Eugene V. Debs,* ed. Joseph M. Bernstein (New York, 1948), pp. 350 ff.
19. Ibid., pp. 370–73.
20. De Leon, *Daily People,* January 5, 1914; *Ultramontanism: The Roman Catholic Political Machine in Action* (New York, 1928), p. 71.
21. *IWW Proc.,* p. 145.
22. "A Plea for Solidarity," *Writings and Speeches of Eugene V. Debs,* p. 373.
23. Theodore Draper, *The Roots of American Communism* (New York, 1957), pp. 393–95; Coser and Howe, *The American Communist Party,* pp. 158–61, 168–74.
24. Bertram D. Wolfe, *Marx and America* (New York, 1934), pp. 5–6.
25. *The Workers Age,* 1936–1939.
26. Coser and Howe, pp. 225, 285–86, 398–401.
27. Earl Browder, *Marx and America: A Study of the Doctrine of Impoverishment* (London, 1959), p. 123.
28. Ibid., p. 47.
29. Ibid., pp. 3–12, 34, 43–47.
30. Marx, *Capital,* I, 708–9.
31. Browder, p. 81.

# bibliography of works cited

Beer, M. *Fifty Years of International Socialism.* New York, 1935.

Bell, Daniel. "Marxian Socialism in the United States." *Socialism in the United States,* I, ed. Donald D. Egbert and Stow Persons. Princeton, 1952.

Bellamy, Edward. *Looking Backward: 2000–1887.* Boston, 1890.

Brissenden, Paul F. *The I.WW.: A Study of American Syndicalism.* 2nd ed.; New York, 1957.

Browder, Earl. *Marx and America: A Study of the Doctrine of Impoverishment.* London, 1959.

Brownson, Henry F. *Orestes A. Brownson's Early Life.* Detroit, 1898.

Brownson, Orestes A. "Abolition and Negro Equality." *Brownson's Quarterly Review* (1864). This article appears also in *The Works of Orestes A. Brownson,* XVII, 537–60.

——. "Abolition Proceedings," *Boston Quarterly Review,* I (1838), 473–500. This article also appears in *The Works of Orestes A. Brownson,* XV, 63–85.

——. "Address to the Workingmen." *Boston Quarterly Review,* IV (1841), 112–27.

——. "Conversations with a Radical." *Boston Quarterly Review,* IV (1841), 1–41.

——. "Democracy and Christianity." *Boston Quarterly Review,* I (1838), 444–73.

——. "Democracy and Reform." *Boston Quarterly Review,* II (1839), 478–517.

——. "A Discourse on Lying." *Boston Quartely Review,* III (1840), 409–20.

——. "Grund's Americans." *Boston Quarterly Review,* I (1838), 161–92.

——. "Introductory Statement." *Boston Quarterly Review,* III (1840), 1–20.

——. "The Laboring Classes." *Boston Quarterly Review,* III (1840), 358–92, 420–510.

——. "Literary Notes." *Boston Quarterly Review,* IV (1841), 390–93.

——. "Norton's Evidences." *Boston Quarterly Review,* II (1839), 86–113.

——. "Our Future Policy." *Boston Quarterly Review,* IV (1841), 68–112.

——. "The Political State of the Country." *Brownson's Quarterly Review* (1873). This article also appears in *The Works of Orestes A. Brownson,* XVIII, 520–35.

——. "Rights of Women." *Boston Quarterly Review,* II (1839), 350–78.

——. "Slavery-Abolitionism." *Boston Quarterly Review,* I (1838), 238–66. This article also appears in *The Works of Orestes A. Brownson,* XV, 63–85.

——. "Specimens of Foreign Literature." *Boston Quarterly Review,* I (1838), 433–44.

——. "Tendency of Modern Civilization." *Boston Quarterly Review,* I (1838), 200–38.

——. "War and Loyalty." *Brownson's Quarterly Review,* (1846). This article also appears in *The Works of Orestes A. Brownson,* XVI, 1–25.

——. *The Works of Orestes A. Brownson,* ed. Henry F. Brownson, 18 Cols. Detroit, 1885–87.

# Bibliography

Christman, Henry. *Tin Horns and Calico: A Decisive Episode in the Emergence of Democracy*. New York, 1945.

Cochran, Bert. *American Labor in Midpassage*. New York, 1959.

Cole, G. D. H. *A History of Socialist Thought*. 5 Vols. London and New York, 5 Vols. 1953–60.

Commons, John R., et al. *A Documentary History of American Industrial Society*. 10 Vols. Cleveland, 1910–11.

——. *History of Labour in the United States*. 3 Vols. New York, 1918, 1934.

Coser, Lewis and Irving Howe. *The American Communist Party: A Critical History (1919–1957)*. Boston, 1957.

David, Henry. *The Haymarket Affair*. New York, 1936.

Debs, Eugene V. *Writings and Speeches of Eugene V. Debs*, ed. Joseph M. Bernstein. New York, 1948.

De Leon, Daniel. *Abolition of Poverty*. New York, 1945.

——. *As to Politics*. 3rd ed.; New York, 1921.

——. *The Ballot and the Class Struggle*. New York, 1935.

——. *Flashlights of the Amsterdam Congress*. New York, 1929.

——. *Revolutionary Socialism in the U.S. Congress*. New York, 1931.

——. *Russia in Revolution: Selected Editorials*. New York, 1930.

——. *Socialist Landmarks: Four Addresses*. New York, 1952.

——. "Preface." August Bebel, *Woman under Socialism*, trans. Daniel De Leon. New York, 1904.

——. *Two Pages from Roman History*. New York, 1915.

——. *Ultramontanism: The Roman Catholic Political Machine in Action*. New York, 1928.

——. *Unity: an Address Delivered by Daniel De Leon at New Pythagoras Hall, New York, February 21, 1908*. New York, 1908.

Dorfman, Joseph. "The Seligman Correspondence, III." *Political Science Quarterly*, LVI (1941), 392–419.

Draper, Theodore. *The Roots of American Communism*. New York, 1957.

Emerson, Ralph W. *The Complete Works of Ralph Waldo Emerson*, ed. Edward Waldo Emerson. 12 Vols. Boston, 1903–1904.

Engels, Friedrich. *Herr Eugen Duehring's Revolution in Science*. New York, 1939.

Fitzsimmons, M. A. "Brownson's Search for the Kingdom of God: the Social Thought of an American Radical." *Review of Politics*, XVI (1934), 22–36.

Foner, Philip S. *History of the Labor Movement in the United States*. 2 Vols. New York, 1947–55.

Gay, Peter. *The Dilemma of Democratic Socialism: Eduard Bernstein's Challenge to Marx*. New York, 1952.

George, Henry. *Progress and Poverty*. New York, 1940.

Gerth, Hans, ed. *The First International: Minutes of the Hague Congress of 1872*. Madison, 1958.

Gronlund, Laurence. *The Co-operative Commonwealth*. Boston, 1884.

Haywood, William D. *Bill Haywood's Book*. New York, 1929.

Hecker, Isaac T. "Doctor Brownson and Bishop Fitzpatrick." *Catholic World*, XLV (April 1887), 1–7.

——. "Doctor Brownson and the Workingman's Party of Fifty Years Ago." *Catholic World*, XLV (May 1887), 200–08.

Hegel, G. W. F. *Vorlesungen die Philosophie der Geschichte, Saemtliche Werke*, ed. Hermann Glockner. 20 Vols. Stuttgart, 1928.

Higham, John. *Strangers in the Land: Patterns of American Nativism: 1860–1925.* New Brunswick, 1955.
Hillquit, Morris. *History of Socialism in the United States.* 5th ed.; New York, 1910.
———. *Loose-Leaves from a Busy Life.* New York, 1934.
Industrial Workers of the World. *Proceedings of the First Convention of the Industrial Workers of the World.* New York, 1906.
Jefferson, Thomas. "Notes on Virginia." *The Life and Selected Writings of Thomas Jefferson,* ed. Adrienne Koch and William Peden. New York, 1944.
Kamman, William F. *Socialism in German-American Literature.* Philadelphia, 1917.
Katz, Rudolph. "With De Leon since '89." *Daniel De Leon: the Man and His Work.* New York, 1934.
Kipnis, Ira. *The American Socialist Movement: 1897–1912.* New York, 1952.
Kriege, Herman. "Our Position on the Questions of the Day." *Der Volkstribun,* November 21, 1846.
Kuhn, Henry, ed. *Daniel De Leon: The Man and His Work.* 4th ed.; New York, 1934.
[Lloyd, Henry Demarest]. "The Progressive Movement Abroad." *Progressive Review* (London), I. 1897.
Luntz, Lester. "Daniel De Leon and the Movement for Social Reform, 1886–1896." Unpublished M.A. thesis, Columbia University, 1939.
Marx, Karl. *Capital: A Critique of Political Economy.* Chicago, 1912.
———. *Selected Works,* ed. V. Adoratsky. 2 Vols. New York, 1935.
———. *Selected Writings in Sociology and Social Philosophy,* ed. T. B. Bottomore and Maximilian Rubel. London, 1956.
———. *Value, Price and Profit,* ed. Eleanor M. Aveling. Chicago, n.d.
Marx, Karl and Friedrich Engels. *Briefwechsel.* 4 Vols. Berlin, 1950.
———. *The Civil War in the United States.* New York, 1937.
———. *Karl Marx and Frederick Engels on Britain.* Moscow, 1955.
———. *Letters to Americans: 1848–1895,* ed. Alexander Trachtenberg. New York, 1953.
———. *The Russian Menace to Europe,* ed. Paul W. Blackstock. Glencoe, 1955.
Mayer, Gustav. *Friedrich Engels: A Biography.* New York, 1936.
Mitrany, David. *Marx against the Peasant: A Study in Social Dogmatism.* Chapel Hill, 1951.
Myrdal, Gunnar. *Rich Lands and Poor: The Road to World Prosperity.* New York, 1958.
Obermann, Karl. *Joseph Weydemeyer: Pioneer of American Socialism.* New York, 1947.
*The People.* 1891–1894, 1898, 1899; as the *Daily People.* 1901, 1904, 1905, 1912.
Perkins, A. J. G. and Theresa Wolfson. *Frances Wright: Free Enquirer.* New York, 1939.
Perlman, Selig. *A History of Trade Unionism in the United States.* New York, 1950.
———. *A Theory of Labor Movement.* New York, 1928.
Petersen, Arnold. *Daniel De Leon: Socialist Architect.* 2 Vols. New York, 1941, 1953.
Quint, Howard. "American Socialists and the Spanish-American War." *American Quarterly,* X (Summer 1958), 131–47.
———. *The Forging of American Socialism: Origins of the Modern Movement.* Columbia, 1953.

# Bibliography

Ramm, Philo. *Ferdinand Lassalle als Rechts-und-Sozialphilosoph.* Viennna, 1953.
Ryan, Alvan S., ed. *The Brownson Reader.* New York, 1955.
Sachs, Emanie. *The Terrible Siren, Victoria Woodhull.* New York, 1928.
Saposs, David J. *Left Wing Unionism: A Study of Radical Policies and Tactics.* New York, 1926.
Schlesinger, Arthur M., Jr. *The Age of Jackson.* Boston, 1946.
———. "Orestes Brownson, American Marxist before Marx." *Sewanee Review,* XLVII (July–September 1939), 317–23.
———. *Orestes A. Brownson: A Pilgrim's Progress.* Boston, 1939.
Schlossberg, Joseph. *The Workers and Their World: Aspects of the Workers' Struggle at Home and Abroad.* New York, 1935.
Schlueter, Herman. *Die Anfaenge der deutschen Arbeiterbewegung in Amerika.* Stuttgart, 1907.
———. *Die Internationale in Amerika: Ein Beitrag zur Geschichte der Arbeiterbewegung in den Vereinigten Staaten.* Chicago, 1918.
———. *Lincoln, Labor and Slavery.* New York, 1913.
———. *The Brewing Industry and the Brewery Workers' Movement in America.* Cincinnati, 1910.
Shannon, David A. *The Socialist Party of America.* New York, 1955.
Sherwin, Oscar. *Prophet of Liberty: the Life and Times of Wendell Phillips.* New York, 1958.
Simpson, George. "The American Karl Marx." *American Mercury,* XXXIII (1934), 60–68.
Sinclair, Upton. *I, Candidate for Governor: And How I Got Licked.* Pasadena, 1935.
Smith, Henry Nash. *Virgin Land: the American West as Symbol and Myth.* Cambridge, Mass., 1950.
Socialist Labor Party, *Proceedings of the Ninth Annual Convention of the Socialist Labor Party, (1896).* New York, 1897.
———. *Proceedings of the Tenth National Convention of the Socialist Labor Party.* New York, 1901.
Sombart, Werner. *Warum gibt es in den Vereinigten Staaten Keinen Sozialismus.* Tuebingen, 1906.
Sorge, Friedrich A. "Die Arbeiterbewegung in den Vereinigten Staaten." *Neue Zeit,* IX, Pt. 1–XIV, Pt. 1 (1890–1895).
———. "Erinerungen eines Achtundviersigers." *Neue Zeit,* XVII, Pt. 2 (1899).
———. "Joseph Weydemeyer." *Pioneer Illustrirter Volks-Kalender.* New York, 1897.
———. *Socialism and the Worker.* New York, 1876.
Stalvey, James B. "Daniel De Leon: A Study of Marxian Orthodoxy in the United States." Unpublished Ph. D. dissertation, University of Illinois, 1947.
Stekloff, G. M. *History of the First International.* London, 1928.
Symes, Lillian and Travers Clement. *Rebel America: The Story of Social Revolt in the United States.* New York, 1934.
Timm, John, et al. *Fifty Years of American Marxism: 1891–1941: Commemorating the Fiftieth Anniversary of the Founding of the Weekly People.* New York, 1941.
Turner, Frederick Jackson. *The Frontier in American History.* New York, 1920.
Wittke, Carl. *Against the Current: The Life of Karl Heinzen.* Chicago, 1945.
———. *The German Language Press in America.* Lexington, 1957.
———. *The Irish in America.* Baton Rouge, 1956.

———. *Refugees of Revolution: The German Forty-Eighters in America.* Philadelphia, 1952.

———. *The Utopian Communist: A Biography of Wilhelm Weitling.* Baton Rouge, 1950.

Wolfe, Bertram D. *Marx and America.* New York, 1934.

*Woodhull and Claflin's Weekly.* 1870–1873.

Woodward, C. Vann. *Reunion and Reaction: The Compromise of 1877 and the end of Reconstruction.* Boston, 1951.

———. *Tom Watson: Agrarian Rebel.* New York, 1938.

# Index

# Index

212